Yellow Peril

Books by Pat Anderson

NOVELS
The McGlinchy Code
The Crimes of Miss Jane Goldie
Torrent
A Toast to Charlie Hanrahan
Catalyst

FACTUAL
Clash of the Agnivores
Fear and Smear
Never Mind the Zombies

FOR CHILDREN
The Skyscraper Rocket Ship
The Ceremony at Goreb Ridge
The Brain Thing
The Football Star
Mighty Pete and the
School Bully School
Mighty Pete and the
Trainer Train Trainers

Yellow Peril

THE 'SNP-BAD' CAMPAIGN

Pat Anderson

Snowy Publications MMXV1

Copyright © 2016 Pat Anderson
All rights reserved.
ISBN: 1530650216
ISBN-13: 978-1530650217

To all the bampots at Bampots Utd.

CONTENTS

Preface and Introduction...............ix
1 It's Her Oil......................................1
2 Will You Walk Into My Parlour......14
3 Whodunnit?...................................26
4 Cyberspats..............................39
5 What The Papers *Don't* Say.........51
6 Power To The People!.............57
7 The Makar's New Clothes............67
8 The Sneaky Stuff.....................75
9 Anti-Union Unionists.....................85
10 Austerity Verities......................97
11 Playing The Green Card...............104
12 A Parcel Of Rogues..................112
13 GER-ymandering?.........................123
14 On The QT.................................132
15 Fear and Smear Redux.................139
Notes..145

Preface

I didn't think there would be anything else to say on the topic of Scottish independence after I wrote 'Fear and Smear'. There have been a host of other books about the Independence Referendum, all exposing the dirty tricks employed by the Better Together side. We all looked forward to a rematch, but Nicola Sturgeon herself ruled it out.

A constant theme among Unionist politicians was that it was time to move on. The majority had voted to stay in the UK, so that was that. Except, of course, it wasn't. We subsequently elected 56 SNP MPs, out of 59, to represent us at Westminster and all the indications pointed to the SNP also winning a substantial majority at Holyrood. This frightened the Unionists half to death.

Then came the bombshell. Nicola Sturgeon stated that if England voted, in the upcoming referendum, to leave the EU while Scotland elected to remain, then that would be reason enough to hold another referendum on Scottish independence. What were the Unionists going to do?

With the Labour Party virtually wiped out in Scotland and the Tories a complete irrelevance, there was nothing else for it but to resurrect all the negativity of the Better Together campaign. The Unionists were proactive in this area, spinning negative stories about the SNP almost as soon as the Independence Referendum was over. While recommending that the independence side 'move on', the Unionists pointedly refused to do so.

And that is what this new book is about; the campaign to undermine our elected representatives, both at Holyrood and Westminster, in a desperate attempt to stop an independent Scotland becoming a reality.

As usual, I've got folk to thank for their support and for providing, albeit unwittingly, some of the content of this book. Rev Stu Campbell's Wings Over Scotland website is indispensable for anyone researching the dirty tricks employed against the SNP. I am assuming that the title 'Rev' is a humorous one and have just called him 'Stu Campbell' in the book. If I am wrong, then I apologise.

I also have to mention Mick and the lads at Bampots Utd, who continue to support by blog and my books. It is not unreasonable to say that, without Mick's support, you would not be reading this book. Without the sales he helped generate I would probably have just given up ages ago.

Finally, I make no apologies for much of my material coming from the Daily Record. Although it is no longer the biggest-selling paper in Scotland, the Record is still Scottish Labour's biggest supporter in the media. It was also instrumental in pushing 'The Vow' and is probably the biggest offender when it comes to an anti-SNP agenda.

I do apologise, though, for the state of the CONTENTS page. No matter what I seem to do it just doesn't look right.

Introduction
Labour's Love Lost

On Question Time on October 29th 2015, a member of the Edinburgh audience asked if Jeremy Corbyn would make any difference to Labour's fortunes in Scotland. Kezia Dugdale, the current leader of Scottish Labour, took the opportunity to regale the audience with a quick party-political speech. She said:

> We are in terrible trouble; I recognise that. It's why I went for the job. Because I believe the values of the Labour Party are as relevant now as they have ever been. Believing in the potential of people and using the power of government to realise that potential. That's the Labour way. I want to build a fairer, more equal country and I think that, over the next few weeks and months, you'll see a Labour policy platform coming forward which will inspire you once again.

Even a couple of years before, this speech would have been met with resounding applause. On this occasion, however, Ms Dugdale's rousing rhetoric was met with nothing but complete silence. David Dimbleby and the panel sat, looking around in obvious embarrassment; such a thing had never happened before. There were no 'boos' or other noises of antipathy; neither were there any mumblings of disbelief nor derisory, ironic laughter. There was just silence.

So low had the Labour Party's stock in Scotland fallen that people did not even care about them anymore. It had all been so quick and complete that nobody, least of all the party itself, really understood what had happened. A member of the Question Time audience, however, had an answer.

After a few comments from the panel and the audience, David Dimbleby pointed to 'And you, sir'. The man he chose was an ordinary-looking individual wearing a blue shirt. When he spoke, his accent easily placed him as originating from Southern England. He had a very interesting take on things.

> I think it's plain that the Labour Party lost Scotland, firstly, because when they had a huge majority in Westminster they ignored Scotland and took the Scottish MPs for granted, and thought they were always going to get 50 MPs up here. And, secondly, they did the Tories' dirty work during the referendum campaign. Simple as that!

When the man was finished speaking the audience responded with rapturous applause, showing that almost everyone agreed with his assessment. It certainly looked as if it was going to be a lot more difficult for Labour to win back the hearts and minds, or even the trust, of the Scottish people than Kezia Dugdale seemed to believe.

A few months earlier a general election had taken place, to select MPs for the Westminster Parliament. Indications had shown that no party was going to gain an overall majority and there would have to be negotiations for anyone to form a government. The situation in Scotland, however, was totally different. The SNP was on course to increase its number of representatives at Westminster dramatically, with some estimates going as high as 45 MPs.[1]

So how did Scottish Labour respond to this unprecedented political change? Well, unfortunately for them, they were so bereft of ideas that they reverted to what was a default position for many of them. It was a strategy of sorts that many in the party remembered from their student days.

Anybody that was at university or college in the 1980s will remember a particular type of student that seemed to be ubiquitous then; for all I know, they still are. These characters dressed differently from the rest of us, spoke differently from the rest of us and even behaved differently from the rest of us. They might speak to you while in a tutorial class or you might even bump into one in your kitchen in the hall of residence; when it came to socialising, though, they tended to stick together and exclude all others. None of these people were ever seen at the students' union; they always went elsewhere. At Stirling they tended to go to some exclusive nightclub in the Kings Park area.

As you no doubt will have guessed, these characters were all upper-class and kept themselves almost exclusively apart from everyone else. Needless to say, when it came time to vote for Student Union President and Vice-President, a couple of these folk stood as Conservative candidates, with all their friends campaigning for them. With a single policy of abolishing the students' union completely, they had not a hope in hell of ever being elected.

On election day you would be faced with a plethora of candidates, of all political shades and none. There would be stalls set up everywhere and you would be accosted left and right by members of various parties, while independent and joke candidates would wander about, thrusting their manifestos at every passer-by. They would use any trick to get your vote; citing friendship, shared interests and even the fact that you still owed them a fiver. One political party, however, stuck to the same tactic year after year; a tactic that, sadly, never seemed to work. This was the Labour Party.

Walking past the Labour Party stall you were greeted with the same old argument every time: 'The Tories are going to get in and the only way to stop them is to vote for the Labour candidate!' Everybody laughed at them and went off and voted for somebody else.

Fast-forward thirty years and those student politicos are now running their respective parties. Unfortunately, their imaginations have not developed much during those intervening years; especially in the Labour Party. That is why, in the 2015 General Election, the best that Labour could offer the Scottish electorate was that not voting Labour was going to let the Tories in. Unfortunately, it worked as well as it had in those 1980s student elections.

Gordon Brown had thrown himself back into the limelight during the referendum with his notorious 'Vow' and he seemed determined to play a part in the General Election. He was one of the ones warning us that unless we voted Labour then we would have a Conservative government.[2] It was a desperate card to play and he probably knew that as much as everyone else.

Rather ironically, while Labour was telling us that a vote

for the SNP was a vote for the Tories, the Conservatives decided to use pretty much the same idea in England. Their pitch was that voting Labour would let the SNP make all sorts of outlandish demands, since Miliband would depend on the support of the SNP to form a government. Posters were produced showing Ed Miliband in Alex Salmond's breast pocket.[3] No words were necessary since the English public had been told for years by the press that the whole of Scotland was living off English taxpayers.

The object of Tory attacks changed after Nicola Sturgeon impressed everyone on television debates. It seemed that the Tories were now prepared to accept that Sturgeon was an effective leader of her party and not Salmond's puppet. Thereafter it was Nicola Sturgeon that had Miliband in her pocket or dancing on the end of strings.[4]

Labour's response to these attacks was to take the moral high ground and refuse to get involved in smear campaigns. They were going to stick to policies and nothing else.[5] In Scotland, however, Labour was not just fighting for seats; it was fighting for its very life. Scottish Labour leader, Jim Murphy, was not as squeamish as his English counterparts. He decided to jump off his Irn Bru crate straight into the gutter.

Remembering his (many) years in student politics, Murphy, of course, told us that if we did not vote Labour, then the Tories would get into power. There was a slight change in this strategy in that not only did we have to vote Labour but we were to specifically avoid voting SNP. Murphy elaborated upon this in a decidedly nasty way, regurgitating the old, old myth of the SNP's vote of no confidence in 1979 ushering in eighteen years of Tory rule.[6]

The fact of the matter was that the Labour Party was living on borrowed time in 1979. Since the General Election of October 1974 various losses in by-elections had left Labour in a minority and it relied on a pact with the Liberals to stay in power. A general election was going to have to be called before the end of 1979; an election that everyone knew was going to end badly for Labour. With the 'Winter of Discontent', rising unemployment, rising inflation and the embarrassment of having to go, cap in hand, to the IMF and the cuts in spending that entailed, the Labour Government did not have its problems to seek. All the vote of no confidence did was hasten the end. If anything, it was a mercy killing.

Labour, though, had a trump card to play in 2015; the Sun. Rupert Murdoch's paper north of the border was supporting the SNP, as it had in the 2011 Holyrood election. The Sun in England, meanwhile, was all for the Tories. To many in the Labour Party this was a cynical ploy to help the Tories into government.

This theory was certainly supported by the fact that the Sun, on both sides of the border, had refused to support Scottish independence in 2014.[7] Now, here was Murdoch throwing the weight of the paper with the biggest circulation in Scotland behind the SNP. It was hardly surprising that many were sceptical.

And so we had the strange situation of the Scottish Sun telling us to vote SNP, while the English edition tried to scare voters into voting Tory with bloodcurdling tales of 'the SNP running the country'.[8] Andrew Nicoll, political editor of the Scottish Sun, denied that there was any cynicism behind their support for the SNP but it was simply a case of 'two distinct editorial positions from two distinct, editorially-diverse newspapers'.[9] Anyone who believed that probably still puts a carrot out for Santa's reindeer!

In truth, though, it is difficult to gauge how much influence the media have on elections; or on any formed opinion, come to that. The man that throws his dinner at the TV whenever Shabnam appears on Eastenders does not get angry because he happened to read negative stories about Muslims in the Daily Mail. It is more likely that he reads the Daily Mail because it agrees with the opinions he already has. And so it is with political parties; people tend to drift to the newspaper that agrees with their voting preferences. An obvious case in point is the Sunday Herald, which reported an 111% increase in sales when it came out as the only paper to support Scottish independence.[10]

Furthermore, newspapers are pretty much in terminal decline in Scotland, as in the rest of the world. 2014 figures show the Scottish Sun at 260,000, with the Daily Record at

219,500.[11] These figures, however, are small beer when you compare them with the glory days when the Daily Record could shift three-quarters of a million copies a day.[12] Even free newspaper, the Metro, has seen its circulation fall.[13] This huge, general decline in circulation casts more doubt on the ability of newspapers to influence opinion.

Even the idea of people choosing newspapers to fit their own viewpoint can have cold water poured on it. It is hardly a representative sample but my dad and his friends buy the Scottish Sun for two reasons only: it has a good racing section and it is the cheapest newspaper around. None of them care, or are even aware of, which party the newspaper supports, or where it stands on certain issues; coverage of the day's race meetings is all they ask!

Much more concrete was the counter-claim by SNP supporters that Scottish Labour was in bed with the Tories. After all, had they not stood with the Tories to fight against Scottish independence? It was a damning indictment as far as those campaigning for independence were concerned, as was the fact that Labour was working with the Tories in five Scottish councils.

In 'Fear and Smear' we encountered Stirling Council's Labour/Conservative coalition's machinations against the celebration of the 700th anniversary of the Battle of Bannockburn.[14] We saw how this was not just a local issue but was done in collusion with the Westminster Government, to stress the importance of the Union and diminish any celebration of Scottish patriotism. This, however, was one council; were the others just as bad?

It should be pointed out that the SNP is actually in coalition with the Tories in East Ayrshire[15], while the coalition councils in East Renfrewshire[16] and Edinburgh[17] involve Labour and the SNP working together. Council coalitions are not always reflective of national politics and, even though the councillors are members of political parties, much can hinge on how individual personalities are viewed both in the chamber and in the community. In East Lothian, for example, a major consideration in the election and the subsequent coalition negotiations was to do with individuals rather than parties.[18] National politics hardly even entered into it.

It is difficult, then, to see Labour's collapse in Scotland purely in terms of a perception of them as 'traitors'. East Lothian elected an SNP candidate to Westminster in 2015 but it is entirely possible that the next council elections will result in an anti-SNP vote again, due to the local personalities involved. On a national level, there were certainly those that bandied the words 'traitor' and 'quisling' about during the election campaign, but that is scarcely proof that such viewpoints caused Labour's collapse in Scotland.

Looking at the election results in England[19] provides an interesting insight into what happened to Labour. Both Labour and Conservative show an increase in their votes, by 3.6% and 1.4% respectively. The biggest losers were the Liberal Democrats, down a whopping 16% from 2010. The party with the biggest increase was UKIP, whose vote jumped by 10.7%. Effectively, you can actually see how the votes of 2010 have moved around, mostly at the expense of the Liberal Democrats. The same voters, essentially, have voted again in 2015, though this time many of them for a different party.

This has been the Labour Party's take on things as well and their report on why they lost the election, 'Emerging from the Darkness…', focuses on swing voters.[20] As the report sees it, Labour needs to reinvent itself in order to win back the middle ground.

Turning to Scotland and results are markedly different from those of England.[21] Every party has lost voters, apart from the SNP, UKIP and the Green Party. UKIP's share has risen by 0.9%, the Greens' by 0.7 and the SNP's by a staggering 30%. Again, one can see how previous votes have been realigned but, in this instance, such a conclusion does not tell the whole story. Unlike in England, where the turnout had increased from 2010 by less than 1%, the percentage of the electorate actually voting in Scotland had jumped from 63.8% to 71.1%.[22]

In 2010 the turnout in Scotland was 2,465,722. Of this 1,035,528 voted for Labour, while 491,386 voted SNP.[23] In 2015 2,910,465 turned out to vote, meaning an extra 444,743 voters.[24] This time, 1,454,436 voted SNP. In 2010, 1,974,336, or 80.1%, of the votes cast did not go to the SNP.[25] In 2015, that figure changed to 1,456,029; a difference of 518,307. Adding that to the SNP's 2010 total only gives 1,009,693. It is a simplistic conclusion to draw, but a fair one nonetheless, that practically all of those 444,743 extra voters turned out to vote SNP.

So, who were these extra voters? Unfortunately, nobody has looked into the demographics of the election yet but it is possible to make a few observations. A list of the worst places of deprivation came out in 2002[26]. I tried to find a more up-to-date one but failed. My searches, however, show that the areas listed in 2002 are still well down at the bottom of the pile economically. I doubt that anyone would argue with my using this 2002 list:

Glasgow Shettleston
Glasgow Springburn
Glasgow Maryhill
Birmingham Ladywood
Manchester Central
Camberwell and Peckham
Glasgow Bailleston
Liverpool Riverside
Hackney South/Shoreditch
Bethnal Green and Bow

The Glasgow areas above are in the parliamentary constituencies of Glasgow East, Glasgow North East and Glasgow North. It is a rather worrying trend that the lower down the social scale you go, the less likely people are to vote. The 2015 election was no different[27] and, in fact, the turnout at all ten of the constituencies listed above were below the national average.[28] It is worth looking at the results in the poorest Scottish constituencies in detail and comparing them with those of 2010.

CONSTITUENCY	CHANGE IN TURNOUT	CHANGE IN SNP VOTE	CHANGE IN NON-SNP VOTE
GLASGOW EAST	10,253	16,159	5,906
GLASGOW N/E	8,448	17,818	9,370
GLASGOW N	7,309	16,080	8,771

It can be easily seen, as in practically the whole of Scotland, that extra voters came out and put their X next to the SNP candidate. Since these constituencies are areas of high unemployment, it is relatively safe to assume that these extra voters were predominantly Class E in the NRS social grade classification system. This conclusion, of course, could quite well be wrong, but it tallies with the demographic study of those that voted in the Independence Referendum. As the Daily Record states, the report showed that 'Yes had majorities among people who classed themselves as working class, people at the bottom of the earnings scale and people in rented social housing.'[29] It is reasonable to assume that those that had voted YES in the Referendum also voted for the SNP in the General Election.

One argument against this is that the turnout for the Referendum was much higher than that for the General Election.[30] In the Referendum, however, it was not just YES supporters that turned out *en masse*. The study of the demographics of the Referendum also pointed to the fact that Protestants were more likely to vote NO than Roman Catholics.[31] This is not to say that there was a straight religious divide in voting; on the contrary, there simply were not enough Catholics in Scotland to account for the huge YES vote.

The figures for Protestants voting NO was probably skewed by those in the Orange Order, whose desperation to keep Scotland in the Union was more inspired by the worry about being disconnected from Northern Ireland than any love for Westminster. Once the Union was saved, many working-class Orangemen probably went back to their normal indolence when it came to voting. That would remove a huge chunk of the electorate from voting in the General Election. In this scenario the idea still holds that the socially disconnected, who had voted YES in the Referendum, came out to vote SNP in the General Election.

A huge underclass has grown in the UK since the 1980s, members of which are totally detached from the society around them. Their lives are ones of poor diet, poor education and poor health. Many struggle with depression and, consequently, cannot see the point in working, education or voting, for that matter. In the schools where these folk live teachers struggle with pupils with no ambition and a grim acceptance of a pointless existence.

Vilified as lazy, shiftless and endlessly scrounging off the state, these people have become an easy scapegoat for all society's ills. If they are not being demonised they are paraded for entertainment on television shows like Jeremy Kyle, Benefits Street and The Scheme. Little wonder that such folk feel marginalised and excluded from the democratic process, indeed, from society in general.

We have already seen that 444,743 extra voters turned out all over Scotland and it is extremely tempting to see those extra voters as coming from the ranks of the disengaged and disaffected. I am more than tempted and believe that future, in-depth analysis will show this to be the case. The SNP's triumph in Scotland is unique and unprecedented in UK electoral history and, therefore, cannot be explained in the usual fashion.

Although this massive swing to the SNP is something new, the reasons behind it are not. It is a return to an old-fashioned kind of politics, where people vote for a party they think is going to improve their lives, rather than choosing the least bad of a bad bunch. The same phenomenon is beginning to appear in England, albeit in a different direction entirely.

It is easy to mock UKIP, and many people do, with its rather backward-looking agenda of Britain leaving the EU and going out to reclaim its rightful place in the world. Apparently, the erstwhile British Empire is waiting to welcome 'Bwana' back with open arms! As well as wanting to return us to a world of £ s d and measuring everything in bushels, firkins and furlongs, UKIP has become the party of anti-immigration and, inevitably, anti-immigrant sentiment. The party denies this, of course, but, as many wags and comedians have pointed out, it often seems as if the more racist and anti-immigrant it appears, the more UKIP's vote rises. And risen it certainly has.

In 2015 UKIP pulled in 3,611,367 votes, an impressive 14.1% of the total, and only the vagaries of the UK electoral system stopped them from gaining more than the solitary seat they won.[32] It might well have only one seat but a party with that many electors behind it cannot be ignored. It is entirely probable that if Britain is still in the EU in 2020 then UKIP might do in England what the SNP has done in Scotland. Even if the UK does vote to leave Europe, the party will still have massive appeal, given its other policies.

And therein lies the huge difference in direction that Scottish politics has taken compared to England. Voters in Scotland are looking for positive solutions; those in England are simply playing the blame game. Tory voters blame people on benefits for everything that has gone, and is going, wrong, while those voting UKIP seek to pass the blame onto the EU and immigration. And Labour? Well, Labour voters in England are merely doing the usual and trying to keep the Tories out. As for the Labour Party itself, there is really only one direction in which they are prepared to point the finger.

On January 20th 2016, Margaret Beckett presented the long-awaited, and dreaded, report into Labour's disastrous results in the 2015 election. It had already been leaked to the press so there were few surprises in it. Amid much beating of breasts and *mea culpa*s, one point stood out:

> The collapse in Scotland made it impossible for us to be the biggest party and the Liberal Democrat collapse enabled the Tories to gain an overall majority and keep us out of power.

It is a bit like the end of a Scooby Doo episode; if it weren't for those pesky Nats we would have succeeded! The truth is that even if Labour had won every seat in Scotland, it still would not have had enough seats to trouble the Tories. The Labour Party, however, are not ones to let the facts get in the way of a deeply-held conviction. And so, as well as looking to win back those English floating voters in 2020, Labour was going to have to deal with the SNP. It did so the only way it knew how; the same way it fought the Independence Referendum and the General Election in Scotland.

The media in Scotland followed the same agenda and

methods; especially the large section that supported Labour. Sadly, this was nothing but business as usual. The 'Fear and Smear' evident in the Referendum campaign was still apparent during the General Election and beyond. It seemed that the Scottish media was disinclined to follow its own advice. After the referendum resulted in a NO victory, everyone desiring Scottish independence was told to 'move on'. With a majority SNP government in place at Holyrood and Scotland being virtually wholly represented by the SNP at Westminster, the Scottish media refused to 'move on'. In fact, they were determined to do all they could to undermine the Scottish Government and our SNP MPs in London.

With nothing at all to offer the electorate, Scottish Labour and its friends in the media continued a campaign of negativity. 'SNP BAD!' was the watchword and it was going to be thumped into us until we came to our senses and went back to the Labour Party.

Yellow Peril

1
It's Her Oil

On 8th May 2015, not long after the General Election, the Daily Record had a shocking story about two aircraft carriers being built at Rosyth for the Royal Navy. It appeared that the company building the ships, the Aircraft Carrier Alliance, made up of Ministry of Defence and engineering companies Babcock, BAE and Thales UK, was hiring East European workers, to the detriment of Scottish ones.[1]

This, however, was not some Daily Mail-type rant about foreigners 'coming over here' and stealing our jobs. What was actually happening was that Scottish workers were being laid off and Eastern Europeans brought in to replace them at a lesser rate of pay. These new workers had to work long hours for about two-thirds of the wages that their Scottish co-workers were getting. It was a scandalous exploitation of cheap labour.

The best part of a year later, on the 28th January 2016, the Daily Record ran another story. This time it was about shipyard workers protesting at labour from Poland and Romania being brought in to work long hours on the cheap.[2] Obviously, nothing had been done in the eight months since the Record had first brought it to our attention.

As usual, there was a section underneath the article for comments and one person was pretty definite who was to blame for this scandal. He said, 'What is STURGEON doing? She wants open flood gates and let them all in with open arms. You were warned. Vote UKIP.'[3] (I have corrected two errors with spelling and punctuation.) Nobody else commented and the Record made no such accusation, but the implication was clear and this was a common theme in our media. The Scottish Government was to blame; even when it was not.

In February 2014 David Cameron had made a statement on North Sea oil:

> This week I will take the Cabinet to Scotland where we will set out how the UK Government can maximise the benefit of North Sea oil and gas to the UK economy for decades into the future, giving a vital boost to local communities and families across Scotland.
> I promise we will continue to use the UK's broad shoulders to invest in this vital industry.[4]

A Westminster source put it more succinctly. 'You might argue Scotland couldn't afford it on its own.'[5] The message could not be clearer; only by staying in the UK could the future of North Sea oil be guaranteed. Westminster's 'broad shoulders' would be there to protect Scottish jobs and communities.

Fast-forward to the end of the year and things had changed dramatically in the oil industry; the price of oil had fallen drastically. There were various global factors at play to cause this fall and it affected every oil producing nation, with the possible exception of Saudi Arabia, which had more than enough financial resources to ride out the crisis.[6]

The reaction of Unionists was, rather predictably, one of gloating. Lord Foulkes, for example, said in the House of Lords, 'Isn't it a good job we voted No in the referendum?'[7] He, and others, gleefully pointed to the falling oil prices as proof that an independent Scotland would have been bankrupt. This, of course, ignores the fact that, in the event of a YES vote, it would have taken a couple of years at the very least for Scotland to be fully independent. Their gloating was premature, given that the price of oil could easily have shot up again before an independent Scotland began to receive tax revenues from it.

As things were, it looked as if the oil industry in Scotland was facing collapse, with a devastating effect on the communities that relied on it. Still, there was no need to worry unduly; the Victor Mature-like physique of Westminster would be there to 'shoulder' the responsibility and ensure that nobody suffered too much. Unfortunately, 'Samson' Cameron did not have that in mind when he spoke in 2014. The Tories are firm believers in market forces and when things go wrong they do not see it as their job to try to ameliorate the situation; unless you happen to be a banker, that is.

Throughout 2015 the price of oil remained low and oil companies had to make cuts in operational expenses. This, of course, meant job losses and, as we moved into 2016, more shedding of employees was predicted.[8] Calls were made for George Osbourne to cut taxes on oil to help boost the industry and avoid job cuts, both from the industry itself[9] and from the Scottish Government.[10]

Remarkably, fingers started to be pointed at the Scottish Government by unions and, of course, by the Labour Party, whose MSP Jackie Baillie claimed that the SNP was in 'utter denial'.[11] Commenters on the Daily Record forum began to resurrect the old label of 'Tartan Tories' for the SNP.[12] Even when it was having a go at Westminster, the Daily Record also had a dig at the Scottish Government, making sure that it did not escape its share of the blame.[13] This from a paper that had been at the forefront of the NO campaign in the Independence Referendum.

So, at the beginning of 2014 we had the Unionist parties telling us that the North Sea oil industry could only be guaranteed to survive under the government at Westminster. Almost exactly a year later we listened to the gloating of Unionist politicians, who thanked God that independence had not happened and that the oil industry was in safe hands. By the start of 2016 the industry was in serious meltdown and about 65,000 jobs had gone. Suddenly, however, the whole crisis was, at least partly, the responsibility of the Scottish Government! And the finger-pointing did not stop there; not by a long chalk.

For years the media had been full of stories of how the NHS was in crisis. The Coalition and the Tory Government that came after were determined to make massive cuts in the

NHS; ostensibly in the name of efficiency. Even before the 2015 election it was obvious that things were going disastrously and were going to get much worse.[14] It was one of the items that Labour had to address in its post-election navel gazing; how did it fail to get the message across that the NHS was under threat?

The Labour Party in Scotland, on the other hand, dispensed completely with the introspection and just went on the attack.

Kezia Dugdale, at the beginning of 2016, had the following observation to make at Holyrood:

> The delivery of NHS services depends on having motivated and well-supported staff.
> But this week the scale of the pressure on our NHS because of SNP cuts and mismanagement was exposed.
> The fact that the NHS lost more than 287,000 days because of staff stress reveals the pressure our health service is under.
> Our NHS is at breaking point and under-pressure staff are crying out for help.[15]

This was an extremely disingenuous argument. The fact was that, for a number of years, the pressure on the NHS in England was increasing so much that staff everywhere were having to take time off due to stress-related illnesses.[16] The situation was just as bad in Wales, which, rather unfortunately for Kezia Dugdale's argument, was under Labour control.[17]

For years there has been concern that the NHS is being privatised by stealth.[18] The argument is that the Tories' healthcare cuts have nothing to do with efficiency and everything to do with profits for big business, which practically funds the Conservative Party. Whatever the reason for the cuts, one thing is certain: cuts in England and Wales affect the amount that the Scottish Government can spend on healthcare.

The Barnett Formula is based on spending in England and Wales, so if there are cuts made by Westminster the grant received by Holyrood reduces accordingly. There are no stipulations on how this grant should be spent; it is up to the Scottish Government to decide. So when Kezia Dugdale demands that more money is spent in hospitals and on recruiting more nursing staff, she is essentially asking the Scottish Government to change its priorities and take money from one area to give to another. Scottish Labour never bothers to specify which area should suffer.

While Kezia Dugdale was demanding more money for extra nurses, Dr Miles Mack, chairman of the Royal College of General Practitioners (Scotland), was calling for more GPs to be recruited.[19] This, naturally, was pounced upon by opposition parties, with the Labour public health spokesman saying, 'This SNP Government has no clear vision of primary care or the role of GPs for the medium to long term.'[20] Again, nobody was prepared to suggest where this redistribution of funds should come from, or which other services should suffer to provide it.

The Daily Record's take on Dr Mack's demands was to point out that the RCGP had, for two years, been demanding that 11% of the NHS budget be spent on GPs.[21] The Scottish Government had announced 100 new training places for the following year, but Dr Mack was concerned that these places would not be taken up. An ordinary GP was wheeled out to provide an explanation,

> The worry is general practice is not seen as an attractive career. There are a lot of unfilled GP vacancies. There will reach a tipping point if the workload seems to be rising more and more.[22]

One person, in the comments section, came up with what he thought was an obvious solution:

> The main problem in the GP service is lack of qualified personnel. So the easiest answer is to increase the salaries of GPs in order to encourage more recruitment.

Just like everyone else, however, he failed to suggest where this extra money was going to come from.

The minimum a GP in Scotland could earn at the start of

2016 was £55,551, rising to a maximum of £83,617.[23] Details on how long it takes to become a GP vary depending on where one looks. The idea that it would take you thirteen years[24] is belied somewhat by the experience most of us probably have of seeing GPs that are definitely under the age of 30. Another suggestion that it requires 5 years at university, 2 foundation years and then 3 years vocational training would appear to be a more reasonable estimate.[25]

Certainly, a junior doctor, starting out after five years at university, was on a starting pay of £23,205[26] but this compared favourably with a secondary-school teacher, who, after five years as a student, would start on £22,416 after April 2016.[27] It can, of course, be argued that junior doctors have to put in long hours and are under the same stresses that Kezia Dugdale claims that nurses face. It is difficult to see how Dr Mack's demands that money be taken from hospitals to be given to GP practices would ameliorate this situation. The end result would be even less people going into medicine as junior doctors and, consequently, less possible recruits to become GPs.

Again, comparing those going into medicine with those going into teaching, very few, if any, teachers can look forward to earning anything like £55k at any point in their careers, never mind before they are thirty. A GP's top salary of £83k, meanwhile, will only ever be attained by a head teacher; even then, he or she would have to be in charge of a school approaching the size of Holyrood Secondary in Glasgow. It is difficult to see where the problem lies in recruiting GPs. Teachers have just as much, if not more, paperwork to do and have to face bolshie, and often violent, teenagers on a daily basis. That is far more stressful than anything a GP has to put up with.

Both doctors and teachers these days have to do further study and pass various courses, at their own expense, if they want to climb the greasy pole to higher positions and higher salaries. There is one major difference, however, in medicine; the courses of study and assessments are far more rigorous and exacting. Apparently, this is to separate the wheat from the chaff and ensure that only the best go on to become specialists or GPs.[28] Even the entrance qualifications to do medicine at university can be prohibitive. The result of this is that we do not have enough doctors and have to recruit from other countries, where entrance qualifications and training is possibly not as stringent. This defeats the purpose of the whole exercise.

Perhaps, rather than shouting and demanding more money, Dr Mack and his organisation should look at widening the opportunities to become a doctor. Doctors recruited from abroad do an excellent job in our NHS so a study should be made of their training and entrance qualifications and adjust our own to be the same. This could quite well open up the profession to young people for whom £55k a year would be a salary worth pursuing.

Even more demands were being made on the Holyrood coffers when a new organisation, calling itself Action for a Safer and Accountable People's NHS in Scotland (ASAP-NHS), was set up.[29] A leading light in this pressure group was Labour MSP Neil Findlay, who was subsequently to achieve infamy for calling Nicola Sturgeon 'a liar' in the Scottish Parliament.[30] Another two were NHS whistleblowers Rab Wilson and Dr Jane Hamilton.

Rab Wilson told his tale of how, when asking too many questions, he was 'fitted up, framed and accused of bullying, harassment and intimidation'.[31] He was apparently even suspended from his post for carrying out his own investigation. Rather unfortunately for the agenda of the Labour Party and the Daily Record, Mr Wilson's problems happened in 2006, when Labour was in charge at Holyrood.[32] (Where was Neil Findlay then?)

The other whistleblower, Dr Jane Hamilton, told of how managers refused to listen to her concerns about patient safety. The Daily Record does not go into details but Dr Hamilton was a consultant psychiatrist at St. John's Hospital in Livingston, working in a unit where women with mental health problems after giving birth were helped. Not only did Dr Hamilton work in this unit; she was actually in charge of it,[33] which puts rather a different slant on the story. She also claimed that the health board had been trying to gag her, which was strange since she was never out of the newspapers.[34]

What ASAP-NHS was calling for was an independent watchdog, similar to that currently operating in England. Again, one has to wonder why Neil Findlay saw no need for this when his own party was in power. It also has to be said that the independent regulator in England, known as Monitor, has not exactly been covering itself in glory.

At the end of 2014 the CEO of one of England's largest NHS trusts resigned, citing Monitor's 'blame-based culture' for driving him out.[35] This 'blame culture' of Monitor was evident in February 2016 when the watchdog accused locum medical staff of 'ripping off the NHS'.[36] In fact, NHS trusts were hidebound by restrictions placed on them by the Government about how many permanent staff they could employ.[37] This meant that they were forced to hire agency staff and, since the demand was far outstripping the supply, many of these staff went to the highest bidder.

Is this what ASAP-NHS wanted for Scotland; a regulatory body looking for people to blame instead of providing answers? Such regulatory bodies, by their very nature, just pile more pressure onto staff. Her Majesty's Inspectorate of Schools, for example, constantly makes recommendations without any clue, or care, about how they should be implemented. It also fails to take account of environmental and social factors. Demanding that a school improves its pupils' attainments in Maths usually come from being compared to another school in the area full of well-fed, clean, aspirational, middle-class children. Failure is laid at the door of the staff, rather than on society in general. This is what would happen with a regulatory body for health boards. There was also the matter of what such a body would cost.

The Scottish Government was being assailed for larger shares of limited funds, while the Labour Party took the side of every interest group going, even though giving them all what they wanted would mean taking money not just from the NHS budget, but from other areas as well.

One such area could be education and, as early as 2012, Scottish Labour had called for an end to free university education in Scotland. Johann Lamont declared that it was 'not sustainable'.[38] It is tempting to agree with the reasoning behind this, which says that tax payers should not be subsidising the well-off to go to university. Things, however, are not as black and white as that.

It is true that the majority of university students come from more well-to-do backgrounds but that does not mean that their parents are, by any means, rich. Middle-class parents could struggle just as much as working-class ones to pay tuition fees, effectively denying many youngsters a place at university. Means-testing does not always work out fairly, as thresholds do not take account of parents' outgoings. Even the children of rich parents can suffer. There were quite a few cases back in the 1970s and 1980s where rich parents were unhappy with the choices of their offspring and refused to pay up. (Some of these students were forced to take their own parents to court.) Are such youngsters to be denied their choice of further education or subject just because their parents have money? Such a situation would be just as discriminatory as young people from a poorer background being stopped from going to university.

While pursuing this policy of denying tertiary education as a right, Scottish Labour, rather glibly, accused the Scottish Government of underfunding primary and secondary education. Kezia Dugdale claimed, in February 2016, that the SNP Government wanted to cut the education budget by £130m.[39] The Scottish Government, however, does not fund schools directly; it is the councils that are responsible for that. What Kezia Dugdale was actually referring to was the Scottish Government not allowing councils to raise council-tax levels, which, Labour argued, effectively amounted to making cuts.

For years the Scottish Government had frozen council tax, mostly with the agreement of COSLA, the Convention of Scottish Local Authorities.[40] The deficit was made up by a grant to the 32 local authorities. Financial responsibility for the police and fire services was now out of the hands of local councils, since they had been made into single units, under the control of Holyrood. This was purely an exercise in saving money and absolved councils of the responsibility of having to either make cuts or divert funds from elsewhere.[41]

One would have imagined that freezing council tax and providing grants to make up any shortfall would have been anathema to the SNP. After all, the SNP were arguing for full fiscal autonomy for the Scottish Government; something that they appeared to be denying to local authorities. The truth was, however, that this system was always meant to be temporary. The aim of the SNP was to abolish the council tax altogether and replace it with something better. In fact, this was not just some promised, long-term aim; the SNP had already attempted to change local taxation.

The attempt to introduce a local income tax in 2008/09, by the minority SNP Scottish Government, was stymied on two fronts. Only the Liberal Democrats supported the new tax, while the Labour Party ridiculed it completely, and the Budget was defeated in January 2009.[42] There was also the problem that councils cannot levy income tax so the Scottish Government would have to administer the tax itself. This, of course, would trigger a commensurate reduction in the Barnett Formula grant; effectively countering any benefits.[43] Not surprisingly, the whole idea was dropped.

Now, suddenly, Scottish Labour was all in favour of raising extra cash by putting income tax up by 1p. This was not instead of council tax but was designed to be a supplement to safeguard services.[44] The poorest-paid would have to pay the tax as well but would be able to claim some sort of rebate amounting to £100.[45] It all sounded needlessly complicated and would probably cost a fortune to administer, nullifying any benefits.

There was also another thing that all the critics of the Scottish Government's funding of local authorities tended to ignore: the councils were not underfunded at all. In fact, a report has shown that the opposite was the case and that Holyrood had actually been slightly *overfunding* local authorities.[46] If there was not enough money for education in council budgets then it was a fault with those councils' budgeting, not with how they were being funded by the Scottish Government. in fact, most Scottish councils were up to their eyes in debt and spending about half of their revenues servicing this debt.

Jackie Baillie, as she always did, attacked the Scottish Government over the huge debts that councils were paying back, blaming the council-tax freeze for the need to borrow.

She said:

> They're (the Scottish Government) forcing councils to borrow more and are therefore amassing a level of debt per household which is eye-watering, and the Scottish government is equally responsible for that ultimately.[47]

The truth was, however, that councils had been building up debts since well before the council-tax freeze. The Labour-controlled Scottish Government gave councils full control over their borrowing in 2004,[48] and the councils followed Holyrood's lead in putting everything on the never-never. While the Labour Scottish Government piled up massive debts for councils and health boards across Scotland, sometimes signing contracts that were going to have to be paid for nearly a hundred years,[49] the councils themselves were taking advantage of LOBO loans,[50] which ended up landing them with huge interest repayments. It is these loans and contracts that are causing councils to have to spend much of their income on debts; not the council-tax freeze. Somebody obviously pointed this out to Jackie Baillie since she did not mention the debts again after 2015.

Nobody at all in Scottish Labour made any suggestions about how councils should work within their budgets; all they demanded was that the Scottish Government handed over more money. At the same time, their comrades at Westminster were helping to ensure that the SNP had even less money to play with. Rather than vote against the Westminster Government's austerity measures, Labour MPs were frequently instructed to abstain.[51] This would, of course, have an effect on the block grant given to Holyrood, reducing the amount the Scottish Government had to spend. The subsequent attacks on the SNP about schools and hospitals, therefore, by Scottish Labour seemed remarkably hypocritical.

And it was not just for social matters that money was being demanded from the Scottish Government. On 5th January 2016 the Daily Record had one of its usual puff pieces about how great it was that some Scottish folk had actually done something. This time it was the film industry that Scottish folk had graced with their presence; more specifically, the movie Star Wars: The Force Awakens.[52] And not only had Scots been involved in this one Star Wars movie – they had been involved in them all. Aye, wha's like us?

One of those involved in the latest Star Wars movie was Tommy Gormley, who had been co-producer. The Daily Record mentioned this man on quite a few occasions; making sure that we all knew who he was and how important he was. Then, in the middle of February, the paper finally dropped its bombshell. Gormley was looking for money.

Scotland is already being used by major filmmakers, such as when Glasgow's George Square featured prominently in World War Z. Gormley, however, said that Scotland was missing out due to the lack of a dedicated film studio.[53] Among all his banging on about tax breaks, UK booms, every studio in London booked and lack of ambition in Scotland there was no mention at all about what was in it for us. What did Scotland have to gain from spending a fortune on some film studio other than prestige? At a time when hospitals were struggling and people were relying on foodbanks, this character Gormley had some nerve.

Also showing some nerve was the Daily Record, which was obviously trying to somehow guilt-trip the Scottish Government into spending on this expensive nonsense, with nothing to gain but some kind of bragging rights. To make a Scottish studio attractive to big film companies, the tax concessions offered would have to be greater than those attainable elsewhere. The only ones making money would be the film companies and the Daily Record would be first in line to accuse the SNP of having wasted public cash. Scottish Labour would have a field day as well.

Labour, and the Tories, got the chance to really point the finger at the SNP when it came to the damage caused by the flooding throughout parts of the UK during the winter of 2015/16. Westminster announced a package of £50m to help victims of the floods on December 29th and opposition parties in Holyrood demanded to know how the Scottish Government was going to spend its share, accusing ministers of being 'glued to their seats'.[54]

On 9th January Nicola Sturgeon announced £12m of

funding to help flood victims. There was to be a £5m fund for local authorities to repair damaged infrastructure and every household, business and charity affected by flood waters would receive a £1,500 grant each.[55] Even this failed to satisfy the critics of the SNP.

Only two weeks later, the Sunday Post was accusing the SNP of taking credit for funding that was being provided by Westminster.[56] The way things were being portrayed, however, it looked as if the UK Government was handing over this money out of the goodness of its heart. The fact was that the extra money was being allotted by Westminster due to further damage caused by storms Eva and Frank; Scotland was simply getting its share under the terms of the Barnett Formula.

In truth, the SNP was not taking credit for providing the funds but was explaining how those funds were going to be spent. Even that was criticised; this time by right-wing pressure group the Tax Payers Alliance. It seemed that the £1,500 promised by Nicola Sturgeon was three times what was being offered in England. A statement said that help for flood victims 'should be determined by the extent of damage suffered rather than which side of Hadrian's Wall they happen to be on'.[57]

This sort of viewpoint takes no account of the fact that the Scottish Government is entitled to spend its money as it sees fit. It has long been a desire of the English right wing that Scotland be treated as a region of England, rather than a separate country. The statement by the TPA betrayed this desire, as did the way the Westminster Government dealt with the extra powers promised in 'The Vow'. It is time to look at this in detail.

2
Will you walk into my parlour...

'The Vow', as the new powers promised to the Scottish Government came to be known, was an illegal manoeuvre by the Unionist side in the Independence Referendum, coming as it did only days before the actual vote. Be that as it may, the fact was that Scotland was still part of the UK and it was incumbent upon the SNP to get the best deal possible.

Almost as soon as the Referendum result was announced, David Cameron rushed to link more powers to Scotland with English Votes for English Laws, much to the fury of Gordon Brown. Brown levelled the accusation that 'on the morning after the referendum the Conservative party stopped thinking about Scotland and started thinking only about the Conservative Party.'[1] It was a valid point, but the counter-argument could be made that Brown was only thinking about the Labour Party, which often relied on Scottish members to get bills approved at Westminster. It seemed that Scotland was way down the list of priorities for both parties.

EVEL was a main part of the Tories' manifesto in the 2015 General Election[2] and, given how much English voters have been fed the lie that their taxes pay for Scotland, it probably influenced many to vote Conservative. Subsequently, even before agreement had been reached on what shape the Scotland Bill should take,

Cameron's EVEL system became law.[3]

For years the right-wing press, as well as many in the Tory Party, have been calling for the Barnett Formula to be scrapped. The story was that it was unfair to the rest of the UK, especially England, and even Lord Barnett himself wanted it done away with.[4] The rush to make EVEL law raised hopes that the time was finally at hand.[5] David Cameron, however, had made it plain in 'The Vow' that the Barnett Formula would be remaining,[6] much to the chagrin of many English Tories.

The Smith Commission deliberated, consulted and finally drew up recommendations and the Scotland Bill was put before the House of Commons. The SNP, however, was not happy with it and it looked as if the Bill might end up running out of time and not be passed. The Daily Record was blazing.

> Moan, moan, bitch, bitch, whinge, whinge. Their response has been as negative as it was predictable. A cynic might argue that the SNP don't actually want those new powers because it makes them more accountable to the people of Scotland.[7]

David Mundell, the Scottish Secretary by virtue of being the only Scottish Tory MP, followed up on this diatribe at Westminster.

> The reality is the powers that are being delivered to the Scottish Parliament will make it the most powerful devolved parliament in the world.
> But rather than tell us what they'll do with those powers, it's grievance and grudge.[8]

Labour MP Ian Murray joined in the blame game by claiming that the SNP was 'looking for any excuse with the fiscal framework to delay further powers for Scotland'.[9] The accusation was that the SNP was playing politics, not wanting the Scotland Bill to succeed. Quite what the accusers believed the SNP hoped to achieve with this policy nobody was able, or willing, to say.

Politicians and the media paraded all these extra powers for Holyrood as if to say to the SNP, 'This is what you wanted!' But the truth is that it was not. It is what those that voted NO wanted; or, rather, what they were promised if they voted that way. As Unionists on newspaper forums never tire of reminding us, 55% voted to remain part of the UK and the SNP had to work within this framework. Presumably everyone wanted to get the best deal possible; or did they?

After the 2015 General Election, the Daily Record had this to say in its editorial column:

> This newspaper is proud to call itself Scotland's Champion. In everything we do, we endeavour to represent what we believe is in the best interests of the ordinary people of Scotland.[10]

One would infer from that statement that the Daily Record expected the Scottish Government to do what was 'in the best interests of the ordinary people of Scotland'. This point cannot be stressed too much. The Daily Record was claiming to want what was in the best interests of the people of *Scotland*; not the people of *England*, nor the people of the *UK*. It was the interests of the people of *Scotland*, and *Scotland* alone that were supposed to be paramount. And yet, the Daily Record did nothing but try to undermine the Scottish Government's attempts to serve the best interests of the people of Scotland.

The arguments between the Scottish and Westminster Governments revolved around the block grant to Scotland. With its main eye on the right wing in its own party, as well as right-wing voters in England, the Westminster Government, understandably, was looking to reduce the amount of the grant by as much as it could. The Scottish Government, equally understandably, was looking to get the best deal it could for Scotland.

Although David Cameron claimed, in 2014, that the Barnett Formula would be maintained, this turned out to be a complete lie. Under the provisions of the Scotland

Bill the block grant would be linked to the Scottish economy, instead of that of the UK. Politicians always have to be looking toward the next election and, with UKIP snapping at its heels, the Tories needed to be seen to be throwing a bone to the right wing in England. Many in England are under the impression that they have been subsidising Scotland for decades; Cameron and his government needed to be mindful of this and try to appeal to this part of the electorate.

The SNP's argument was that any substantial reduction in the block grant would be detrimental to Scotland. They pointed to the fundamental clauses that were agreed upon right at the beginning of the Smith Commission. These were Principles 5 and 6 of the Agreement, which said that any powers devolved to Scotland should:

5) not cause detriment to the UK as a whole nor to any of its constituent parts'
6) cause neither the UK Government nor the Scottish Government to gain or lose financially simply as a consequence of devolving a specific power.[11]

As Alex Salmond pointed out, this meant that Scotland should not suffer financially because of having powers devolved. Westminster wanted to use the latest Government Expenditure and Revenue Scotland (GERS) figures, taking them as an average of Scottish revenue and basing the block grant on bringing Scotland's revenue up to the level of those figures. The SNP argued that this was unfair since, in previous years, Scotland's balance was ahead of the UK's, instead of being behind it as it was at present.[12]

With this new way of calculating the block grant, Scotland's economy would not have a chance. If the economy in Scotland were to grow in the future, then the block grant would be cut to the bone to maintain the standard of the 2014-15 GERS figures; effectively negating any benefits. If, however, the Scottish economy was to grow only slightly, while the rest of the UK pulled ahead, Scotland would still lose out, since the grant would be cut again to maintain those 2014-15 levels. Essentially, we would have all of the pitfalls of independence but none of the benefits. As John Swinney put it, 'Heads, the UK wins; tails, Scotland loses.'[13]

The SNP wanted to keep the Barnett Formula as it was, but Westminster argued that this would be unfair to the rest of the UK since Scotland could possibly benefit from a rise in tax income to which it did not contribute.[14] So who was in the right here?

The argument put forward by Westminster was persuasive but the fact remained that all parties signed up to the Smith Commission's Principles, which clearly stated that no part of the UK should suffer detriment because of devolved powers.

The SNP was fighting Scotland's corner, which was, supposedly, what the Daily Record wanted it to do. And yet, this paper, along with most of the rest of the Scottish media, did everything it could to undermine what the SNP was trying to do.

On 2nd February 2016, the Daily Record had this to say:

> They are the two leaders who will decide the future of Scotland. Yet after months of big promises, fiery rhetoric and hard-won compromise, they look set to let us all down. Nicola Sturgeon and David Cameron are on the brink of allowing Scotland's new package of powers to fall at the final hurdle.[15]

That seemed fair enough. They were blaming both sides for not reaching an agreement. Read the article further, however, and the emphasis changed dramatically. 'Until now, the Tory Prime Minister has lived up to the promises extracted from him by this newspaper on the frantic final days of the referendum campaign.'[16]

Ah! Now we were getting to the real nitty-gritty. The Tories were not to blame at all; it was all the fault of those nasty Nats! Just in case that implication was too subtle for us, the Record drove it home with a sledgehammer.

> The SNP have treated the entire Scotland Bill process

with a surly dismissiveness bordering on the dishonest. The party seem terrified of actually being given some of the powers they've campaigned for all their lives.[17]

And there you had it folks. The SNP was deliberately holding back all those extra powers for Scotland, failing completely to 'put the national interest ahead of party advantage.'[18]

The Record, however, undermined its argument somewhat by pointing out what its 'Vow' was supposed to be about:

Scotland would take responsibility for a powerful package of tax and spending decisions while contributing to, and benefiting from, the economic strengths and social benefits of the United Kingdom.[19]

The Tories' planned Scotland Bill would fail in the context of this description. Surely the Daily Record could see that basing the block grant purely on Scotland's GERS would mean us losing out on the economic strengths of the UK? Or maybe they did not want to see. While accusing the SNP of putting party before people, the Daily Record, the Scottish media and Scottish Labour were desperate to see the whole enterprise fail. Why else would they be so keen for the SNP to walk into what was essentially a political trap?

The Tories could not care less about Scottish politics anymore. Their EVEL legislation had effectively neutered Scottish representation at Westminster, whether that representation be Labour, SNP or anybody else. It also helped to keep the Labour Party from ever forming an effective government, since it would have to rely on a much-increased English majority to pass legislation. With the sop to the English right wing in the reduction of the block grant to Scotland, the Conservative Party was sitting pretty.

Labour, meanwhile, was in total disarray. Party members were still arguing with each other about what went wrong in the General Election and what the way forward should be. They had landed themselves with a leader that the parliamentary party neither liked nor wanted and all they could see was a future filled with Tory governments. If they did ever get back into power, they would want to get rid of EVEL as quickly as possible so that they can have the support of the 'Celtic Fringe' once again. They failed, however, to take account of the history of politics in Britain.

When the so-called 'Glorious Revolution' took place in 1688, with James II deposed and William III invited to take over the throne, there were two main factions in both Houses of Parliament. These were called the Whigs and the Tories; the Whigs were supportive of William, while the Tories were all for the legitimacy of the Stuart dynasty. Not surprisingly, the Whigs became the dominant force in politics and remained so for nearly a hundred years.[20]

In the late 18th Century, with the threats posed to the Establishment by the American and French Revolutions, the Tories and the Whigs became more confirmed as political parties; the Tories the party of establishment and law and order, the Whigs that of nonconformity and social and political change.[21]

With the electorate changing during the 19th Century, there was a realignment, producing two new parties; the Liberals and the Conservatives. Although the Conservatives are often called 'Tories', it was, in fact, a new party. The repeal of the Corn Laws in 1846 split the Tories irrevocably and the new Liberal Party contained many erstwhile Tories, while some Whigs moved to the Conservatives.[22]

More changes happened when Joseph Chamberlain and other Liberals crossed the House in protest at Gladstone's proposals for Home Rule for Ireland.[23] Many of these Liberal Unionists moved closer and closer toward the Conservatives and, in many cases, ended up joining the party. The Unionist Party, as it came to be known in Scotland, continued to take advantage of Scottish links with Northern Ireland, although, politically, it was hardly distinguishable from the Conservatives.[24]

The Liberal Party vote in England gradually moved to

Labour, while both Labour and the SNP benefited from the amalgamation of the Scottish Unionists with the Conservatives. The Liberals were never to return to the glories of 1906; they were effectively finished as a force in British politics, having given up their electorate to Labour. The dominant force in Scottish politics, meanwhile, became Labour.

The main lesson to be taken from the history of politics in Britain is that there is no going back. Support for parties changed with changing circumstances and a changing electorate, while the parties themselves were changed by the same forces. By the 1870s the old Tories and Whigs were dead and, even though the labels might persist, two new parties had taken their place. A working-class electorate at the end of the 19th Century led to the creation of the Labour Party, which took over from the Liberal Party as the opposition to the Conservatives with the gradual extension of the franchise to all after the First World War. All of these changes were irrevocable.

And now, politics in Scotland had evolved again. The SNP had taken over from Labour as the dominant force and, as history has shown, this was not liable to change back. The only way Scottish Labour could ever recover in Scotland would be to reinvent itself in the way Tony Blair and Gordon Brown did with Labour in the 1990s.[25] As well as doing that, however, it was going to have to destroy the dominance of the SNP.

Kezia Dugdale's policy of putting an extra penny on income tax[26] was nothing more than a smokescreen for what Labour was really up to. Ostensibly, it was a desperate gambit by a party that had no chance at all of being elected and so would never be called to account. The real concern of Scottish Labour was the Scotland Bill and what the SNP was going to do.

The best-case scenario, as far as Labour was concerned, was that the SNP accepted Westminster's method of calculating the block grant. All Labour needed to do then was to stand back and watch as the Scottish Government ran into more and more trouble financially. Then the SNP could be portrayed as being incompetent and Scottish

Labour, in some new guise, would be ready, and willing, to pick up the pieces. This scenario would also have the added benefit of making Scottish independence seem undesirable. If Scotland could not manage with extra fiscal powers and a block-grant safety net, how the hell would it manage completely on its own?

If the SNP refused to be taken in by Westminster's trap, then Scottish Labour and its friends in the media would be ready to point the finger of blame. Westminster was offering a massive increase in powers for the Scottish Government and, yet, the SNP was turning this generous offer down! As we have seen, this accusation was already doing the rounds in the media.

A key piece of evidence that Labour was pursuing such an agenda was that not one Scottish Labour politician, and certainly none of the nominally left-wing Scottish media, had blamed the Tories for the collapse of negotiations over the Scotland Bill. The Westminster Government had moved the goalposts and was not adhering to either the spirit or the letter of the Smith Agreement. Labour and its friends in the media would rather put the blame onto the SNP, which spoke volumes about what their priorities were.

The cynicism of Scottish Labour was also pointed up by the political consequences of the abandonment of the Barnett Formula. As Charlie Jeffery, Senior Vice-Principal of Edinburgh, emphasised to the Westminster Scottish Affairs Committee, the Barnett Formula and EVEL are mutually incompatible.[27] As long as Scotland's block grant was linked to public spending in England, EVEL was practically unworkable. Since increases or reductions in public spending by Westminster would have a knock-on effect on spending in Scotland, then Scottish MPs would have a right to vote on measures that, ostensibly, were solely the preserve of English MPs.

On the other hand, linking the block grant to the Scottish economy would mean that English legislation had nothing at all to do with Scottish representatives. This would eventually mean less need for there to even be Scottish MPs at Westminster; something that would certainly be to the benefit of the SNP. With less representation at Westminster, the case for Scottish independence would become virtually unassailable.

The SNP's insistence on maintaining the Barnett Formula, therefore, showed that, contrary to what our media would have us believe, the SNP was putting the interests of Scotland before its own, narrow, party interests. Meanwhile, Labour was playing a dangerous game of looking to sentence Scotland to years of economic misery, purely in the hope that it would cause the collapse of the SNP's support. This move could quite easily backfire if the Scottish electorate saw where the blame really lay; with the Tories at Westminster.

On 5th February 2016 the Daily Record had an editorial that, ostensibly, seemed to suggest that they were finally seeing through the Tories' deceit. It said:

David Cameron must abide by his Vow that the devolution settlement will work for Scotland, and if he doesn't, Nicola Sturgeon is right to maintain a hardline stance against it.[28]

The article went on, however, to complain that all the negotiations were being done in secret so that nobody knew what was going on. In fact, the SNP had continually kept us informed about what was going on and what the Tories were up to. The Record, however, said, 'If it's not the case that the Tories are trying to pull a fast one on Scotland, they need to publish hard facts to prove it.'[29]

Essentially what the Daily Record was saying was that they did not believe the SNP and would only believe if David Cameron confirmed it. So much for being a left-wing newspaper! To add insult to injury, the following, snide little comment appeared:

But with a Holyrood election on the horizon, it also isn't beyond the realms of possibility that the SNP pair are happy to stymie a deal for political reasons. Another source for Nationalist grudge and grievance could suit them.[30]

As we have already seen, the abandonment of the Barnett Formula could actually work in the SNP's favour, as long as the Scottish people saw that the blame lay with the Westminster Tories. Labour's best hope lay in the Scotland Bill failing to be passed. Obviously that was what the Daily Record wanted to see too.

At last agreement was reached over the financial framework and the Scotland Bill was going to be able to go ahead.[31] There would be no detriment to Scotland, but the deal would be reviewed in 2022. Rather brazenly, Kezia Dugdale had this to say about the news:

Scottish Labour's position has been clear all along – we would only support a deal that protected the Barnett formula which has benefited generations of Scots. It appears that this deal does exactly that and has our support.[32]

That was hardly the impression we had got in the media.

She went on:

Now that an agreement has been reached every single political party in Scotland must focus on what we can do with these major new powers. The opportunities they provide are huge – we can use the new tax and welfare powers to bring an end to Tory austerity and build a fairer country.[33]

Now that agreement had been reached the emphasis was moved from blaming the SNP for holding up the Scotland Bill to demanding that the Scottish Government used the new powers to end austerity in Scotland. This is a different subject entirely and will be looked at in a later chapter. In the meantime, despite all the plaudits and declarations that they had all been behind the SNP in the negotiations, the fact was that the Scottish Government had achieved the result itself, without help or support from anyone. If anything, everyone had done their best to, if not sabotage, at least hinder the negotiations.

Politics can be a dirty business and it seemed that there were none dirtier than Scottish Labour and its cronies in the media. Pursuing the 'SNP-BAD' agenda, however, was not just about blaming the Scottish Government for everything and undermining its bargaining powers with Westminster. Also, as had been shown during the Independence Referendum, a bit of character assassination never went amiss!

3
Whodunnit?

In April 2015, with the General Election campaign in full swing, the Telegraph newspaper dropped a bombshell. It appeared that Nicola Sturgeon had had a conversation with the French Ambassador, in which she had confessed that she and her party would prefer David Cameron and the Tories to win the election.[1] A civil-service memo had been leaked to the Telegraph, apparently proving that this conversation had taken place.

It was a strange story for a Tory-supporting, right-wing paper like the Telegraph to run. It was obvious that the Tories wanted the SNP to win in Scotland to reduce Labour's influence, so why would they want to diminish the chance of that happening? The story might also undermine the tale being fed to the English electorate that a vote for Labour would lead to the SNP running the show at Westminster. Then again, it was a story that no editor could resist publishing, no matter what his paper's political viewpoint.

Scottish Labour, of course, leaped on the story immediately, with Jim Murphy having this to say:

> This is a devastating revelation that exposes the uncomfortable truth behind the SNP's General Election campaign.
> For months Nicola Sturgeon has been telling Scots she wants rid of David Cameron yet behind closed

doors with foreign governments she admits she wants a Tory Government.[2]

As it turned out, it was Alistair Carmichael, Liberal Democrat MP for Orkney and Shetland and Secretary of State for Scotland in the Coalition Government, who had leaked the memo to the Telegraph. There is no need here to go into the aftermath. Suffice it to say that Carmichael got away with his lies and none of our media bothered to point out what a disgrace the whole thing was. Nobody bothered to apologise to Nicola Sturgeon either!

Also during the General Election came an attack on the SNP candidate for the Ochil and South Perthshire constituency, Tasmina Ahmed-Sheikh. It appeared that Ms Ahmed-Sheikh had previously stood for the Tories and had once been a member of the Labour Party.[3] A Labour spokesperson pounced on this revelation, saying, 'Tasmina Ahmed-Sheikh has held more political opinions than she's had hot dinners.'[4] Changing one's mind in politics, it seemed, was something to be condemned.

Changing political parties has long been an element of UK politics, with many high-profile MPs switching sides. UKIP MEP and founder-member and leader of similar, right-wing party, Veritas, Robert Kilroy-Silk was once a Labour MP. Other former Labour MPs included leader of the British Union of Fascists, Oswald Mosley, whom the Labour Party had been quite happy to accept from the Tories. In later years, Labour was perfectly willing to welcome erstwhile Tories Alan Howarth, Shaun Woodward and Quentin Davies, among others. And, back in the day, Winston Churchill crossed the floor so many times they had to replace the carpet!

It was a rather pathetic attack on Tasmina Ahmed-Sheikh, which showed the desperation of Labour and its supporters in the media. But they were not finished with Ms Ahmed-Sheikh yet. In January 2016 a story appeared detailing how a charity, the Scottish Asian Women's Association, of which Ms Ahmed-Sheikh had been chairwoman, had made very few donations to good causes; only £700 out of £25,000 raised.[5]

The papers were at pains to point out that no illegality or impropriety was being implied on Ms Ahmed-Sheikh's part.[6] The main bone of contention, it appeared, was that the Scottish Government had helped out with the charity's launch, providing Stirling Castle as a venue and helping to pay for the catering. This would have cost the charity £16,000 if it had paid for it itself.[7] Scottish Labour, and the other two main parties, called for an enquiry.

On February 1st, Ms Ahmed-Sheikh tweeted images of apologies that had appeared in the Daily Record and the Herald. They were tiny pieces, tucked away out of sight in the papers, while the online editions did not carry them at all. The Herald's apology said:

> We reported on January 14 that that the 2014/15 accounts for the Scottish Asian Women's Association showed that no donations whatsoever had been made by the charity. This is not the case. In fact, donations were made by the charity in 2015. We apologise for the error.[8]

The Daily Record, meanwhile, was more concerned with convincing us that there was actually no implication in its original article that there had been 'any illegal activity or misuse of public cash'. It apologised by saying, 'We are happy to clarify this and apologise if any inference was drawn to the contrary.'[9]

It seemed as if the whole affair was being quietly, and rather sheepishly, dropped. This, of course, begs the question of why the story was considered to be worth running with in the first place. The fact that these apologies were hidden away and are practically impossible to find on the internet diminishes their impact considerably. The smear was effectively done and the seeds of mistrust were sown. As far as most folk will be concerned, the ostensible lack of an apology means that they will still see Ms Ahmed-Sheikh as completely untrustworthy.

Another SNP MP hit the headlines in October 2015. Michelle Thomson had built up a property business worth

£1.7m before becoming an MP. Apparently, a lawyer involved with her business deals was struck off while another was sanctioned by the Law Society of Scotland.[10] The police were looking into Thomson's deals that these lawyers were involved in.

The impression given by the Daily Record article was that these lawyers were in trouble because of their involvement in Thomson's business deals. That, however, was not the case. In fact, close reading of the article reveals that the police were investigating Thomson precisely because of the involvement of these two lawyers, not the other way around.[11]

Not ones to let the truth get in the way of a good story, the Record wheeled out some of the folk whose properties she had bought to let us all know what an utter bitch Thomson was. Complete details of the people involved were not given, so there is no way of knowing why they did not sell their properties on the open market, or come to some arrangement with their mortgage lenders, all of whom are quite willing to accept nominal payments until you get back on your feet; the last thing they want is a repossession where the likelihood is that they will lose money. Quite telling is the fact that one of the couples still went ahead with selling their property to Thomson's company, even though their solicitor had advised them not to.[12]

It has to be said that Thomson's business deals sound rather immoral, but that could be said about the majority of business deals. It has yet to be shown that she did anything illegal but, in the meantime, she has resigned the SNP whip and currently, at the time of writing, sits at Westminster as an independent. She and her lawyer have expressed a complete willingness to co-operate with the police.[13]

This was not the first time that the media had had it in for Michelle Thomson. Only a matter of weeks before, the papers were falling over themselves in their glee over her e-mail address appearing on a website for organising extra-marital affairs. Ashley Madison, the website in question, had been hacked, and the user database stolen, in July by a group calling itself Impact Team.[14] The group threatened to expose this database unless the parent company closed Ashley Madison and other websites. The company refused to comply and the details of millions of users of the website were released, along with a self-righteous, Mary Whitehouse-like condemnation of them all.

Journalists must have spent days combing the list of names and it is remarkable that the only one they thought worth reporting was that of Michelle Thomson. The Guardian decided that the names and details were genuine, based on the ridiculous premise that a few of those they had had analysed were real.[15] Remarkably, it took a right-wing commentator to set the record straight.

Guido Fawkes, who, as well as running his often extremist blog, writes a column in the English Sun, had a *bona fide* expert look at the details released about Michelle Thomson. His conclusion was that the account was fake and that Thomson had had nothing to do with it.[16] This Guido Fawkes character had nothing to gain politically from this revelation and it tells its own tale that a right-winger like himself was interested in finding the truth, while our more liberal and left-wing press was perfectly content to go along with the smear.

In November it was MSP Sandra White's turn. Like many, White is against the state of Israel's persecution of the Palestinians and has spoken about this on many occasions. Those that support Israel usually accuse those that oppose Israeli actions in Palestine of anti-Semitism. It is a lazy and unjustified accusation, usually levelled by people that themselves display abject Islamophobia.

Also like many, White is sickened by our country being embroiled in conflicts in the Middle East and has started to question the veracity of what we are told is the reason for these wars. People are beginning to suspect that powerful, capitalist interests are at play and that wars are being orchestrated by arms manufacturers and banks in order, not just to make money, but to increase their control over us all. It is not a new argument but more and more people are coming to believe it.

White tweeted an image that reflected this idea; an image that showed piglets, wearing labels depicting them as the UK, ISIS, Al Qaeda, the USA, Israel and Boko Haram, suckling at the teats of a large sow with the word 'Rothschild' written on it.[17] The picture was obviously anti-capitalist but, almost immediately, White was accused of being anti-Semitic.

White had to apologise for the tweet and explained that she found it 'repellent and offensive' and that her tweeting of it had been 'accidental'.[18] This immediately raised the question: how could anyone re-tweet an image accidentally? It is possible, indeed probable, that White was not talking about a slip of the finger or the like, but something entirely different.

As can be seen above the image itself, it was originally tweeted by one Charles Frith.[19] There is a website devoted to warning everyone about this loathsome individual,[20] which suggests that many have fallen victim to retweeting Frith's filth, in the mistaken belief that it has a different meaning. The website explains what kind of character Frith is; an anti-Semite, Nazi apologist and Holocaust denier. The website begs everyone not to retweet anything from this person as, by doing so, you are helping to promote his vile agenda.

It would appear that Sandra White was guilty of nothing more than a misunderstanding. The image she tweeted is not in itself racist, unless one is prepared to scrutinise it with a magnifying glass and see the bank with the Star of David on it. After she tweeted the image, White probably found out where the original tweet had come from and immediately deleted it. She apologised and it would have been expected that everyone would move on. Some folk, however, were unwilling to let it go.[21]

The instigator of the petition to have White sacked, Jonathan Manevitch, is a signatory to Yachad, an organisation that seeks to establish a two-state solution in Palestine.[22] Obviously he is no hard-line conservative, making excuses for everything Israel does. Unfortunately, however, he has been taken in as well and, if successful, will lose a supporter of everything he stands for.

A point worth noting, and to which we shall return later, is the contention by the website about Charles Frith that retweeting anything at all of this individual's, no matter what it is, is inadvertently helping to give the character publicity and promotion. It is hard to disagree with this assertion, which most people would find reasonable and, as I say, it is worth bearing it in mind.

Racism became a recurring theme. A Dundee councillor, Craig Melville, who also happened to be an aide to SNP deputy leader, Stewart Hosie, was accused of sending racist and foul-mouthed texts to a colleague.[23] He was immediately suspended from both the party and from his job with Hosie. Subsequently, he was also reported to the Standards Commission by the leader of Dundee's SNP-led city council.[24]

This is all fair enough and if the man is proven to be guilty, then he deserves to lose his position as a councillor and his place in the SNP. What is unpalatable about the story, however, is the undisguised joy shown in reporting it. In fact, the Daily Record could hardly wait to tell us about another alleged case of racism; what it called 'SNP Race Row No. 2'.[25]

This story was all about a group of SNP members taking the huff at a meeting in Coatbridge because their preferred candidate was not selected for a new post. It is all standard stuff at a local politics level, with cliques forming and lots of 'he said…she said…' accusations flying around. The chosen candidate, Imtiaz Majid, was apparently upset at the wee clique storming out and said something about his colour being an issue. This annoyed the group that was in the huff and Majid has seemingly claimed that he has been subjected to racist abuse on previous occasions.[26]

This playground behaviour can be witnessed at meetings of any political party at a local level, as everyone knows each other, with all the friendships and enmities that that entails. The reason why this petty feud had been picked up on was because one of the members of the clique that went in the huff was Julie McAnulty, who happened to be a list candidate for the coming Holyrood elections.

When McAnulty refused to sit next to Majid at a council meeting, asking to be seated elsewhere, the Daily Record portrayed this as further proof of racism, instead of the petty disagreement that it obviously was. An 'SNP source' was quoted as saying, 'It is appalling the party are dragging their heels. With such a serious allegation you'd expect McAnulty to get her whip withdrawn.'[27] No prizes for guessing which side of the argument that 'source' was on!

McAnulty told the National that the accusations against her were a 'stitch up' because she was leading an enquiry into a £30m-a-year deal between North Lanarkshire Council and a housing firm. This firm, apparently, had links with many politicians in the area.[28] The majority of our media, however, decided that this story was not worth investigating. The story was reported in a few places in July 2015[29] but had been subsequently pretty much ignored. Perhaps that had something to do with the fact that Labour politicians were involved as well as SNP ones.

Concentrating on McAnulty made more sense since she was an ally of the SNP MP for Coatbridge, Chryston and Bellshill, Phil Boswell, whom the media was determined to 'get'. Boswell had been accused of hypocrisy since, as the Daily Record put it, he 'benefited from a legal tax avoidance scheme after campaigning against them.'[30] This, however, was a complete lie.

Boswell had, in fact, received an interest-free loan of £18,308.82 when he worked for American energy company, Phillips 66, before he became an MP. He pointed out that such a way of being paid was common practice in the energy industry.[31] He had made no effort to hide this payment, having declared it to the Parliamentary Register of Members' Financial Interests.[32] At any rate, having benefited from a practice is no bar to believing that such a practice is wrong and immoral and calling for it to be abolished. For example, many of the politicians demanding that Oxford and Cambridge be more open to working-class students have benefited from a middle-class upbringing and an Oxbridge education themselves. That does not make them hypocrites.

The label 'hypocrite', moreover, is, in fact, hypocritical

itself, coming as it does from Scottish Labour, Liberal-Democrats and Conservatives, as well as the Scottish media. None of these groups have been exactly forthcoming in condemning the use of interest-free loans at Rangers Football Club. On the contrary, many have gone out of their way to, if not justify it, then at least excuse it.

Phil Boswell is also, at time of writing, being investigated for not properly declaring his directorship of Boswell and Johnston Ltd.[33] The investigation was prompted by a complaint by a Liberal- Democrat MP, which suggests that there had been folk poring over every detail of SNP MPs in order to find some kind of discrepancy. The improper declaration will probably turn out to be ruled to be an oversight, to the chagrin of our main Scottish political parties outside the SNP. No doubt they are already seeking other things to report.

While no explicit accusation was made of impropriety on the part of Boswell, no such scruples were involved when it came to Natalie McGarry, SNP MP for Glasgow East. As well as being involved in a highly-publicised Twitter feud with writer JK Rowling, about which more later, McGarry was also reported as being involved in the scandal of money, amounting to several thousands of pounds, being missing from the funds of Women for Independence.[34]

Natalie McGarry was one of the founder members of Women for Independence, a group devoted to encouraging more women to take part in the electoral process, especially the Independence Referendum. The group has continued to work ever since toward getting more women involved in politics. In 2015 the group discovered that £30,000 in donations were unaccounted for. McGarry admits that the bookkeeping at WFI was not all it could be and she handed over a 'four-figure' sum to the organisation to help sort out the 'shambles'.[35]

According to the office manager of Scottish Government minister, Humza Yousaf, Shona McAlpine, the whole thing was just another case of internecine quarrelling. McAlpine was one of the original founders of

WFI, along with McGarry, and claimed to have resigned from the group 'because of the bullying and horrible attitude of the egos in it.'[36] She was also adamant that Natalie McGarry was innocent of any wrongdoing.

McGarry offered to co-operate fully with any police investigation. The police, for their part, had not discovered any evidence of criminality yet.[37] That, however, did not stop our Fourth Estate from hounding McGarry into resigning the SNP whip.[38] Nor did it stop our media from digging around desperately trying to find other accusations it could make against McGarry.

In October 2015 McGarry went to Syria on a fact-finding mission. Scores of 'Cyberbrits' were straight onto Twitter, demanding to know where the cash for the trip had come from and accusing her of using tax-payer's money. McGarry denied all the accusations and stated that the funding of the trip was in the House of Commons register of members' interests. By the start of December, the Daily Record had decided to get involved in the argument.

The Record's Torcuil Crichton claimed that there were no entries at all for Natalie McGarry in the register of members' interests.[39] Just in case we missed the implication that McGarry was a crook, Crichton made sure to mention the money missing from Women for Independence. We were left in no doubt at all as to what we were supposed to think of McGarry.

As things turned out, the Westminster staff had simply not got around to processing McGarry's entry in the register and it appeared later that day. No apology was ever published by the Record and no amendments were made to the story online. As Wings Over Scotland pointed out, the original story was left as it was for anyone searching for Natalie McGarry to find.[40] At first the story could be argued to have been a mistake; afterwards, however, it was nothing more than a downright lie.

Strangely, when it came to stories about financial irregularities, or, then again, perhaps not so strangely, the media were rather reluctant to mention the case of one Kezia Dugdale. Dugdale's constituency party, in East

Edinburgh, discovered that £10,000 was missing from its accounts. Weirdly, and some might say suspiciously, they waited a whole year before getting in touch with the police.[41] Probably they wanted to avoid a scandal during the General Election campaign. Our media no doubt ignored the story for the same reason. It had already been reported in the Edinburgh Evening News in July 2014[42] so there was no possibility of the national press feigning ignorance.

By the time the Daily Record got around to telling us about it, at the end of November 2015, half the money had been found. There were no calls for Kezia Dugdale to resign as leader of Scottish Labour, the way Natalie McGarry had been forced to resign the whip. It seemed that irregularities in Labour coffers were to be treated far differently from those associated with the SNP. Also, Labour members were innocent until proven guilty, while the opposite was true for those in the SNP!

Next in the firing line was Dr Philippa Whitford, SNP MP for Central Ayrshire. The Daily Mail broke the story of how Dr Whitford still worked for her local NHS as a locum surgeon; 'moonlighting,' the Mail called it.[43] She was apparently earning about £500 a day, on top of her MP's salary of £74,000 a year. The article went on to detail the 'hypocritical' earnings of other SNP MPs,[44] showing a
remarkable effrontery, given its support for fat-cat Tory politicians.

To its shame, the Daily Record pounced on the story, quoting the ubiquitous Jackie Baillie of Scottish Labour:

> The fact that Philippa Whitford, on a lucrative MP's salary, can still make an hourly rate in our NHS nearly seven times the living wage shows the real problems in our NHS and how understaffed and under-resourced our health service is under the SNP.[45]

In fact, Dr Whitford had been helping out at Crosshouse Hospital, during the Christmas holidays, due to illness among other members of staff. NHS Ayrshire and Arran was seriously understaffed and was struggling to meet targets to bring down waiting times for operations; a situation that the Daily Record had recently highlighted itself.[46] We have already looked at the UK-wide crisis in the recruitment of medical professionals and NHS Ayrshire and Arran was at the sharp end of this crisis. It was hardly surprising that Dr Whitford had to be called to step into the breach when somebody went off sick. Perhaps Jackie Baillie and the Daily Record would have preferred that more people would have had to wait for their operations, while NHS Ayrshire and Arran slipped deeper into trouble.

Staying with the Daily Record, the paper really scraped the bottom of the barrel with a story in March 2016. The headline screamed:

> SNP Party Members among the 14 MPs who had official House of Commons credit cards suspended after racking up £58,000 worth of expenses debts.[47]

That made it sound as if each MP had spent £58,000, when, in reality, £58,000 was the total. In fact, the highest amount owed by any of the SNP MPs was the £3,446.95 owed by Stewart Hosie. As usual, the Record was twisting things to suit its own agenda.

The Independent Parliamentary Standards Authority (IPSA) issues credit cards to all MPs, who then submit their bills for inspection, along with written justification for their spending. Things are then worked out, IPSA owing MPs money and vice-versa. As an IPSA spokesman said,

> By its very nature the operation of the expenses system means Ipsa often owes outstanding amounts to MPs and MPs often owe outstanding amounts to Ipsa. Outstanding amounts are then repaid.[48]

In other words, owing money on these credit cards is a common occurrence. Quite often, it is IPSA that owes the money to MPs; that, however, did not interest the Daily

Record.

The paper went on to state, '(Natalie) McGarry had £2370 outstanding on February 23, a freedom of information request showed.'[49] One wonders who made that FOI request and why. At any rate, all the article showed was that the Record was willing to go to any lengths to bad-mouth the SNP.

Our last reluctant media personality was not an MP, MSP or councillor, but an ordinary member of the SNP. This individual, whose name was Tommy Ball, had carried out an online campaign against a former SNP colleague, claiming that he was a 'known paedophile' and a 'sexual pervert'.[50] Ball was eventually found guilty and fined £1500.[51]

So why should we be interested in the media reporting of this evil idiot? The answer is simple: our media could not bring itself to admit that this was the work of one individual. Instead, an attempt was made to drag the whole SNP into it. Ball was described as a 'Cybernat', the media's term for folk spouting online abuse against Unionists, which, apparently was co-ordinated centrally by the SNP. The implication was clear; the whole party was to blame, not just this one, obviously demented character. To the media, there was a whole group of users of social media, just waiting for the signal from on high to start dishing out abuse to all and sundry. It is time to move on to the continuing myth of the 'Cybernat'.

4
Cyberspats

The Westboro Baptist Church has an infamy far beyond its base in Kansas and its small membership, which consists of one, extended family. The family all works in the world it purports to hate, giving a large sum of its earnings to the church, meaning that practically all the family's income is tax-free. They believe that they are the only ones that will be saved on Judgment Day; everybody else will burn in Hell. They hate gays, Jews, other religious groups, the military, the American Government and, in fact, just about everybody outside of their own compound. They are not shy in expressing this hatred, traveling all over the USA to picket anything they do not like.[1]

When David Bowie died in January 2016 the Westboro Baptist Church immediately threatened to picket the memorial service that was being planned to take place in New York's Carnegie Hall.[2] As well as this threat, the church also sent abusive tweets to Bowie's family, including messages to his widow, telling her not to follow her husband into Hell.[3] Strangely, our mainstream media did not think this, the subsequent uproar and the collection of thousands of dollars for cancer charities to counter the hatred of the WBC were worth reporting. Instead, they concentrated on another, tenuously related, story.

It appeared that some folk had decided to take to Twitter to condemn Bowie's call for Scotland to 'stay with us' during the Independence Referendum campaign. A few examples were given by the Daily Record, most of them anonymous.[4] Of course, the Record and the rest of the Scottish media screamed, 'Cybernats!' It is worth taking a look at the comments on the Daily Record's article, as more than a few condemned the paper for trying to make political capital out of Bowie's death. For example, one commenter had this to say:

> Some tenuous comments stretched out to blacken the SNP. This is how low the Record will stoop for their desperate labour pals. With this bar set expect some really bizarre stories the closer we get to polling day.[5]

Another cast doubt on the comments themselves, saying,

> Some proof wouldn't go amiss, I've searched Twitter using the alleged "posts" you have stated in this "story" none of them actually appear . . .[6]

Whether or not the tweets were genuine, one thing was certain; the media's obsession with 'Cybernats' had returned; in fact, it had never gone away. Anyone that disagreed with a Unionist was a Cybernat, working to a central, SNP agenda. No wonder some folk got angry on social media! Of course, the usual suspects were paraded in the press as the victims of this vile, online abuse.

Michelle Mone is not, by any stretch of the imagination, what you would call a good role-model for young girls. She boasts about leaving school with no qualifications and has made her money from flogging cleavage-enhancing bras, diet pills and fake tan.[7] This all panders to a certain image of women that many thought had died out: the slim, tanned dolly-bird with big tits and an empty head. It is hardly the sort of self-image that we would want our schoolchildren growing up with.

She also relates how she lied on her CV to get a job with the Labatt brewing company. She rose through the ranks to become the company's head of marketing in

Scotland,[8] which might explain why 'Labatt' is not the first word on everyone's lips when they purchase beer! Mone's lies, half-truths and ignoring of inconvenient facts did not stop with her CV. She claims to have left school at 15, even though the school-leaving age was raised to 16 two years after she was born and says that she grew up in a slum when most slums in Glasgow had already been cleared before her birth in 1971. Other facts are left out in her life story, such as how being married into a well-off family helped when starting her own business, as did re-mortgaging her family home.[9] She has described this

property as a 'wee flat, with no TV',[10] which makes one wonder how re-mortgaging it raised enough to get the business started.

Mone outsourced the manufacture of her bras to China, where it was alleged that the workers toiled in sweatshop conditions. Denying this, Mone said, 'I'm trying to create jobs in Scotland'.[11] Quite how she was doing that by using factories in China she did not explain. A reason for why she was having her products made abroad came from her own lips. While complaining about workers having too many rights, she said:

> I'm from the east end of Glasgow and I am for the people. But there's too much about the people. There's 90 per cent for the employee and 10 per cent for the employer.[12]

All-in-all, Mone was the type of business tycoon that the Daily Mirror and Daily Record would normally have torn to pieces in their pages. She was a vocal supporter of the Labour Party, however, so these particular papers went remarkably easy on her. In 2009 Mone defected to the Tories, a heinous crime, one would have thought, in the eyes of our nominally left-wing press. Again, though, there was no condemnation, no exposés, nothing at all said. Being a Tory was no big deal anymore; there was a new enemy in town.

As early as January 2012 Mone threatened to leave

Scotland if it voted for independence in the mooted referendum.[13] Since the Labour Party had made it plain that it would be campaigning to stay in the UK, Mone was seen as an ally. No matter what she did from that point on she would be in the right as far as our media was concerned. Even taking a seat in the House of Lords as a Tory peer was something to be praised, not condemned.[14]

During the Independence Referendum Mone was constantly bleating about being 'attacked' by Cybernats on Twitter. It is worth pointing out that she never joined the Better Together campaign but merely handed out advice to all of us little people on social media. One tweet said, 'will you stay in scotland if it's a yes? I'm off if it is>I said 2 years ago that I would leave if it was a Yes & stick by it'.[15] It was hardly surprising that she received criticism. As for abuse, it was notable that she was only able to provide one or two examples.

Mone even went on Good Morning Britain to tell Susanna Reid and Ben Shephard how her situation was analogous to a child being bullied at school.[16] She claimed to have reported the abusive tweets to Twitter but that nothing was done and she never heard back from them. The presenters asked why she had not contacted the police and she struggled to answer the question, mumbling things about 'being strong'. Eventually Ben Shephard had to answer the question for her to give her a bit of wriggle room.

Twitter has admitted before that it is not too great at dealing with abuse[17] but one would have thought that if Mone was receiving death threats, as she claimed on Good Morning Britain, she would have contacted the police. She said that she was concerned about children but, in fact, her attitude would have had nothing but a negative impact. Her mumbled excuse that she was 'strong' would obviously send out the message that anyone 'grassing' was weak. At any rate, none of this 'deluge of abuse' seemed to stop Mone from continuing to use Twitter.

On 22nd May 2015 Mone declared to her Twitter

followers that she was leaving Scotland, apparently for business reasons. She could not help, however, having a dig, saying, 'Note all the SNP muppets. I haven't turned my back on Scotland purely biz global commitments. I certainly won't miss u angry, hated, jealous lot'.[18] Such a comment was bound, and probably calculated, to elicit abusive replies. After all, Mone herself was being abusive.

Just over a week later, Mone was back in the press, claiming that she had been driven out of Scotland by the Cybernats. The Daily Record called her the 'bleating bra queen' but the actual article belied this headline and was strictly on the side of La Mone.[19] Her article in the Mail contained nothing but hatred and bile toward the SNP, accusing them of being deliberately divisive and of being like children in the playground in the hallowed corridors of Westminster.[20] It seemed that Mone was perfectly willing to dish it out but did not like receiving it.

As plenty of folk pointed out, Twitter is available in England as well so Mone would hardly be escaping the Cybernats, would she? She had, however, also pointed out that, 'For the first time, I didn't feel safe in Scotland.'[21] This fear, though, had not prevented her from signing copies of her autobiography in Glasgow a few weeks previously.[22] And therein lay the real reason for her constant appearances in the media; she had a book to flog.

Her book had been branded a pack of lies by Mone's ex-husband,[23] an opinion that Mone did not want inspected too closely. Much better that all the focus be on her and what better way than to look for sympathy by making up the usual stories about Cybernats. She used the same tactics later in the year when her appointment to head a Government review into entrepreneurship and small businesses, as well as her being made a life peer, were criticised. Much of the criticism actually came from business leaders[24] and Tories,[25] something that Mone had to counter by playing the sympathy card yet again.[26] For all Michelle Mone professes to hate the Cybernats, she has actually done quite well out of this invention.

When Mone first announced that she was leaving Scotland her tweet said, 'My passion & love will never die for #Scotland'.[27] That was maybe why she entered the House of Lords as Baroness Mone of Mayfair.[28] Perhaps we have yet to hear the full story about why she decided to decamp to London.

A rather more important character than Mone (although the Lady herself would dispute it) was trumpeted in our media as receiving vile abuse from Cybernats. This individual was practically treated as a demigod in the press and was viewed as having an almost papal infallibility; we were, indeed, fortunate that she had decided to come and dwell among us mere mortals in Scotland. The person in question is, of course, the writer, JK Rowling.

Rowling has millions of followers on Twitter and these 'Cyberpotters' cluster around like antibodies, ready to attack anyone that dares criticise their heroine. It matters not what that criticism is, the Cyberpotters treat it all as hostile and run to the press with every little thing. Our press then relates how Rowling 'destroyed' some character on Twitter, usually by calling them a 'death eater' or some such. With devastating wit like that it is a wonder that anyone dares offer any criticism at all.

Not only do the Cyberpotters buzz around, looking for what they call 'abuse', they are not above handing out some abuse of their own.

In 2005 Warner Bros. was working on the film adaptation of Rowling's fourth Harry Potter book, 'The Goblet of Fire'. In the book there is a witch pop band called the 'Weird Sisters' and Warner had decided to feature this group in the movie. The plan was that Jarvis Cocker, of Pulp, and others would make up the band and there were even plans for the release of an album. Unfortunately, there was already a band in Canada, called the Wyrd Sisters, who owned the copyright to the name. Rather than end up in legal wrangles, Warner decided not to name the band in the movie.

The Wyrd Sisters, however, took Warner to court, wanting the band removed from the movie completely.

Their argument was that everyone knew full well what the name of the band in the movie was and they did not want to be accused of stealing a name from a Harry Potter book, when the name was theirs in the first place. The band were even prepared to accept a line in the credits, saying, 'The real Wyrd Sisters live in Canada.'[29] Warners refused and, in the subsequent court case, the big money, predictably, won out.

That, however, was not the only thing that Kim Baryluk, the owner of the name Wyrd Sisters, had to contend with. The Cyberpotters came out in force and Baryluk was swamped with abusive mail and death threats.[30] Strangely, we never heard about this in our media; Rowling, it seems is untouchable. More on that in Chapter 5.

Like Michelle Mone, a lot in Rowling's life story does not add up. A young, single mother on benefits in Edinburgh in the early 1990s would have been lucky to be put in a flat in Greendykes or Muirhouse; Rowling, however, was given a flat in Gardners Crescent, off Fountainbridge.[31] She then moved to another flat in South Lorne Place, which is painted as being one step up from a slum.[32] In fact, at that time gentrification was marching down Leith Walk and many middle-class families had bought properties in the area around Rowling's flat in the late 1980s. The other major point in Rowling's original biography of her writing in a café, relying, like Blanche DuBois, on the kindness of strangers[33] was eventually amended when it emerged that the café had actually belonged to her brother-in-law.[34]

Quite why it is considered necessary to portray this image of abject poverty and misery is a mystery. Rowling's books speak for themselves and sold in their multi-millions because they are well-written and enjoyable; not because anyone feels sorry for the author. Perhaps, however, Ms Rowling's idea of poverty is different from that of the rest of us. She might have been concerned that she would have to send her daughter to the 'local comprehensive'; a fate worse than death, to which Uncle Vernon had been ready to consign poor

Harry Potter.[34]

Like Mone, Rowling supported the Labour Party. Unlike Mone, she continues to do so for what she claims are altruistic reasons. Part of her support for Labour, however, was manifest in wanting to keep Scotland a part of the United Kingdom, which did not endear her to many that wanted independence. Of course, she received some abuse but, then, there are always nutters out there ready to spout bile if you declare an allegiance publicly.

Interestingly, Rowling did not contact the police herself; one of her Cyberpotters did that for her, claiming that she:

> found this extremely distressing and aggressive. Language like this makes me feel unsafe to voice my opinions online and in the independence referendum.[35]

Some more level-headed journalists condemned nutters on both sides[36] but the vast majority of our media ran with the 'Cybernats' line and were determined to pin the blame for any abuse online onto the SNP.

The story did not finish with the end of the referendum and we frequently heard about Rowling being deluged with abuse throughout 2015. This reached a kind of denouement in October of that year when Rowling tweeted her support for the Scottish rugby team. She immediately received criticism and Nicola Sturgeon tweeted the following:

> Note to my fellow independence supporters. People who disagree are not anti-Scottish. Does our cause no good to hurl abuse (& it's wrong).[37]

The press concluded that Sturgeon's intervention proved that Rowling was being abused by Cybernats. In fact, it proved nothing of the sort; Sturgeon would have been well aware that the media would twist anything said and she had to act quickly to calm things down. As usual, no evidence of this purported abuse was provided; all the

Daily Record could come up with was this message to Rowling from 'Wings Over Scotland' blogger, Stu Campbell: 'You don't think we're a nation at all.'[38] Good God! It is surprising that another Cyberpotter did not get 'distressed'!

Rowling's reply was far more revealing than Campbell's, though, of course, nobody bothered to pick up on it. She said, 'I know Scotland's a nation. I live there, you see. I pay tax there and I contribute more than bile there.'[39] What, exactly, was that supposed to mean? It is well known that Stu Campbell does not live in Scotland; was Rowling suggesting that if you do not pay tax in Scotland you should not have an opinion on how it is governed? Or perhaps she was saying that only taxpayers should be able to voice an opinion.

Whatever the truth, it was obvious that the myth of the Cybernat was not going to go away. It was an invention of the media but, unfortunately, it has entered the public consciousness, as is evident from comments on social media and newspaper forums. There is not one shred of evidence for any organised, online campaign; it is nothing more than a lie. Also rather suspect are the claims about celebrities receiving death threats.

This book and 'Fear and Smear' are self-published on Amazon's Createspace, which is probably why I do not receive abuse on Twitter. If my books were more widely-available and more widely-known, I have no doubt that I would be inundated with tweets calling me everything under the sun. It is something that pretty much goes with the territory and most people just accept it or block the perpetrators. Nobody is going to get too upset over some clown with a limited vocabulary trying to make a name for himself. Death threats, however, are another matter entirely.

If I received death threats they would immediately be passed onto the police and others that receive them always do likewise. Alex Salmond received such threats and the police were informed at once; we were also able to see what these threats consisted of in the papers.[40] The same could not be said of the claimed threats against

Michelle Mone and JK Rowling, which undermines those claims more than somewhat. Meanwhile, an incident in England helped to cast even more doubt on our media's ridiculous assertions about Cybernats.

Conservative MP Lucy Allan had voted in the House of Commons to bomb Syria and, understandably, was criticised on her Facebook account and by e-mail. Allan claimed that she was receiving abuse and death threats and posted an example on her Facebook page to prove her point. Unfortunately for her, the sender of the e-mail produced proof that she had doctored it. She eventually admitted this and removed the whole thread from her Facebook page.[41] She has since become a laughing-stock on social media and there have been calls for her resignation.

This sordid little episode should make our media a bit more careful about reporting death threats with little, or no, evidence. This, however, is unlikely to happen in Scotland. The whole agenda of our media is not about support for individuals; it is about attacking the SNP. It matters little to our Fourth Estate whether there is evidence or not; all that matters is that they get people to believe in the Cybernats. In this they have been remarkably successful.

When celebrities die they are generally eulogised to the point of hagiography; John Lennon went from being a sad, old, junkie has-been to a musical genius, Paula Yates from a drug-addled attention-seeker to the voice of a generation and Princess Diana from a neglectful parent, only interested in long holidays and boyfriends to the very model of motherhood. Not everyone, however, joins in the outpourings of grief and some folk refuse to change their opinion of an individual just because he or she has died.

Cilla Black was a pretty anodyne celebrity. Personally, I have always found her voice to be reminiscent of fingernails down a blackboard, while the television shows she presented were really about the contestants and they could have thrown a baboon on to front them with no change in the ratings. She was, however, a harmless enough individual.

When Ms Black died we were bombarded with the usual stuff about 'wonderful human being', 'national treasure' and 'irreplaceable'. Also as usual there were folk that were sickened by all the saccharin guff, who decided to voice their true opinion. This was immediately condemned; probably rightly since there is a time and a place. This condemnation, however, took a rather sinister turn. Actress Frances Barber appeared in the press, having taken to Twitter to blame 'SNP Cybernats' for the criticism of Black.[42]

Barber cited the abuse with which Michelle Mone was 'besieged' and called for the Cybernats to be arrested. As usual, only two examples of the abuse meted out to Cilla Black were cited; one tucked away in a corner and reduced to a practically minuscule size. The main tweet presented said, 'Cilla Black, a Thatcherite who opposed an Independent Scotland. Cant join in the cybergrief.'[43] That hardly sounds abusive. The other tweet, however, was a different matter. It said, 'F- Cilla Black, she supported Better Together, hope she rots in hell.'[44]

It cannot be argued that the second tweet is anything other than abusive. One has to wonder, therefore, why that was not presented as the main evidence instead of the one that contained no abuse at all. There must be a reason why the abusive tweet was reduced in size so as to discourage scrutiny. If you do scrutinise it and search on Twitter, you will find that the account does not match the handle. You will also discover that the account is run by somebody that opposes the SNP.[45] Curious, to say the least. The account of the non-abusive tweet, on the other hand, is entirely genuine.[46] Obviously it was felt that a bit more was needed to convince everyone of how evil the SNP was; hence the other, tiny, fake tweet.

A more vicious slant to the 'Cybernat' hysteria was given by Janet Street-Porter in the Daily Mail. Apparently, Street-Porter was inundated with abuse when she tweeted a picture of herself with a grotesque character, made from a giant ice-cream cone, along with the caption, 'Just met Nicola Sturgeon lookalike out canvassing.'[47] Ironically, Street-Porter then proceeds to practically rip Nicola Sturgeon to pieces, while the comments section displays the very abuse, against Sturgeon, that Street-Porter claims to condemn.

As usual in these cases, not much evidence was provided to show the extent of this 'abuse'. Street-Porter says, 'According to her (Sturgeon's) followers, I am a traitor to my sex, a woman less attractive than Red Rum, a sub-human who should be neutered.'[48] None of that seems particularly abusive; in fact, it is pretty much in line with Street-Porter's initial tweet.

Early in her article, Street-Porter cites the great traditions of political satire, with the likes of 'Have I Got News For You' featuring prominently. I remember distinctly the panellists on this programme making fun of David Blunkett's blindness. I do not remember Street-Porter condemning this; in fact, she has been a participant on the programme. If such mockery is acceptable to her, then she can hardly complain if she is mocked in a similar fashion. She might argue that she is not a politician but she openly made a political comment on Twitter, effectively making herself fair game.

I wonder how the Cyberpotters would react if someone put a grotesque picture on Twitter, claiming that it was JK Rowling. Our media would completely ignore any abuse or death threats handed out by Rowling's supporters. In fact, they would be first in line to scream, 'Cybernats!'

With such chicanery going on it is no surprise that many people no longer trust newspapers and look to online social media for their news. Some of the writers of this social media have been absorbed into the mainstream, so to speak, writing for the two newspapers that support Scottish independence. As things have turned out, however, there is now a growing concern about whether or not these newspapers can be trusted either.

5
What the Papers *Don't* Say

Football clubs are notoriously thin-skinned and it is not unusual, in fact, it is quite common, for them to ban particular journalists when they object to something they have said or written. Football being what it is, supporters are outraged when a rival team does it but rally round their own club when it bans somebody. In the main, however, most supporters of all clubs find it ridiculous and, quite often, amusing.

One Scottish team and its supporters took exception to what a BBC reporter said about them and, as usually happens, the reporter was banned from the club. The BBC responded by backing its reporter and has since refused to send anyone at all to the club's ground.[1] This was only to be expected since most media will support their journalists to the hilt.

The same club did not like an article in the Herald either and demanded an apology, threatening to take the paper to court. There were also rumours that one of the club's directors was going to withdraw his advertising from the paper, seriously affecting its income.[2] The Herald subsequently published an apology for the article, without the journalist's knowledge or consent.[3]

The journalist was understandably angry about the whole affair and resigned. The National Union of Journalists was outraged that the paper had not stood by its reporter and made its feelings known.[4] This anger was compounded by the sacking of Angela Haggerty from her column in the Sunday Herald for tweeting her support for the journalist. The sacking seemed all the worse when it transpired that the editor of the Sunday Herald had had nothing to do with it; it was the editor-in-chief of the Herald group, Magnus Llewellin, who had made the decision.[5]

In the middle of February Ms Haggerty was reinstated and allowed to resume writing her weekly column in the Sunday Herald. Magnus Llewellin said,

> After careful consideration - including a re-examination of the context of her original social media postings - the decision has been made to reinstate Angela as a columnist.[6]

No further explanation was given and one suspects that there were some frantic negotiations going on in the background, particularly with the NUJ. It was too little too late, however; the newspaper group had shown that financial considerations mattered more than the truth.

It is worth noting that the football club itself had not complained about Haggerty, which probably helped influence the decision to reinstate her. It was the fans of the football club that had complained about Haggerty, not the club; this is what prompted the NUJ to accuse the Herald group of 'pandering to the mob'.[7] In fact, it was money, not the mob, that Llewellen had been concerned about and one imagines that a quick phone call to the football club would be made to establish that they had no objections to Haggerty. Graham Spiers was still left hanging out to dry.

The way that a newspaper, in fact, a whole newspaper group, had caved in to pressure due to financial considerations had serious implications for the integrity of our media in Scotland. It also helped to explain much of the behaviour of that media.

In the middle of the summer of 2015 JK Rowling brought Edinburgh traffic to a standstill while having her bush trimmed. Now, stop that sniggering at the back there; it was the huge, 30ft Leylandii hedge, which blocked the view to her house in Cramond, that was being cut back. This operation caused days of disruption, with temporary traffic lights and large tailbacks on the roads in her neighbourhood.[8] Cramond provides a through-road for cars coming from South Queensferry into Edinburgh, which means that it is a busy area with traffic coming over from Fife. The bush trimming, therefore, caused disruption to a lot more folk than just Rowling's neighbours.

This was reported in the English and UK press but was largely ignored by the Scottish media. The earlier stories about the writer buying and then demolishing the house next door to make her garden bigger and getting planning permission to erect huge treehouses, despite the objections of her neighbours, also failed to make much of an impact in the Scottish media.[9] [10]

Rich people are notoriously litigious and JK Rowling is no different, having instigated more than 50 lawsuits against the press.[11] She sued the Daily Mail in 2014 over an article they published, which she claimed had caused her 'distress'.[12] After that episode it seemed that newspapers were afraid to print anything the least bit critical for fear of ending up in court. This was especially true of the press in Scotland, which, with hugely declining sales, simply could not afford to take on somebody with far more financial resources than they had. This, of course, was just a theory; the Herald incident in 2016, however, appeared to confirm that it was fact.

It could be argued that this is not the case and that our media shows no fear or favour when dealing with the extremely rich. An example would be how the owner of Sports Direct, Mike Ashley, has been portrayed recently in the press. The fact is, though, that if you do a search on the online versions of Scottish newspapers and read the articles about Ashley, the papers are actually remarkably circumspect in their attacks. If you read carefully you will notice that they report what *other people say* about Ashley and only attack him in a roundabout way. Even when it comes to the issue of zero-hours contracts, most of the attacks are of a 'he said' 'she said' type.[13] It certainly seems that newspapers have one eye on possible lawsuits when it comes to reporting about the super-rich.

At the end of January, Natalie McGarry, who, you will remember, had to resign the SNP whip after a campaign in the press to practically implicate her in a theft, accused JK Rowling on Twitter of defending 'abusive and misogynist trolls'. The Daily Record's headline immediately told whose side they were on:

> JK Rowling DESTROYS ex-SNP politician on Twitter after she's accused of 'supporting misogyny and abuse.[14]

The article was extremely sycophantic, saying that Rowling 'has become known for her brilliant social media ways' and calling her the 'reigning queen of Twitter'. McGarry, meanwhile was referred to as 'the politico'.[15] As well as this sickening stuff, the paper did its usual job of twisting things as much as possible.

Remember the story, in Chapter 3, of Sandra White and her inadvertent tweeting of a Charles Frith cartoon? There was a website we looked at that begged people not to use any of Frith's material, since this was, albeit unconsciously, giving Frith the oxygen of publicity and displaying an accidental support of his vile racism. It was this that McGarry was accusing Rowling of, as Stu Campbell pointed out.[16]

McGarry had said that Rowling had defended 'abusive misogynist trolls', while Rowling kept repeating, 'Show me where I have defended misogyny and abuse, please'.[17] Just as the media do, Rowling was twisting McGarry's words into meaning something totally different.

The 'abusive misogynist troll' was an individual calling himself Brian Spanner. Stu Campbell provides some examples of this character's contributions to Twitter. Be warned; his language is abusive to say the least.[18] Rowling had thanked this character for raising money for her charity, which prompted McGarry to attempt to point out to her what kind of individual Brian Spanner was. It is worth noting that the Record did not mention Brian Spanner once in its article; probably out of fear that readers would search for him and make up their own minds.[19]

Disingenuously, the Record goes on about how calm Rowling was, politely asking the same question over and over. She could well afford to be so calm; the Cyberpotters were already on the attack in the background. McGarry received more than 75,000 notifications on Twitter from Rowling's supporters.[20] Rowling did not call off her dogs until she had forced an apology from McGarry by threatening to sue her.[21]

That our media lied and manipulated this story for its own ends is bad enough; they also, however, ignored the real story altogether. It appeared that Rowling's connection to Brian Spanner went much deeper than a simple tweet thanking him for making a donation to her charity. Rowling has millions of followers on Twitter but only follows 281 accounts.[22] One of these accounts is that of Brian Spanner, who is apparently also
followed by a lot of high-profile people, including Muriel Gray, who says he is 'hilarious'.[23]

In case anyone reading this is unaware of how Twitter works, if you follow someone, it means that you get to see all of their tweets on your own account. Any claims by JK Rowling that she was unaware of Brian Spanner's vile tweets would, therefore, be nothing more than a lie. That is, unless journalist Derek Bateman is correct and somebody else runs the Twitter account on Rowling's behalf. But, then, Bateman is candid in admitting that he has to be careful about what he says:

> As I've been writing, I was very conscious of the threat of legal action. On a blog. In a free country. I've never experienced that before since I started blogging. And it feels uncomfortable.[24]

And that pretty much summed things up. While accusing the SNP and the Cybernats of stifling debate, our media is afraid to say anything critical about rich supporters of the UK. This is what really stops proper debate in our media; the mega-rich can say whatever they like and support sheer filth written by others with not a word of condemnation in our press. Ordinary people, meanwhile, cannot say anything at all without being accused of being 'abusive Cybernats'.

The most depressing aspect of all this is that it is not only the Unionist press that lives in fear; the papers that ostensibly support Scottish independence are terrified as well. Neither the Sunday Herald nor the National dug too deeply into the Twitter spat between Rowling and McGarry, even though the truth was all over online social media. The only possible reason is fear of being sued. This conclusion is made all the more plausible by the fact that both newspapers come under the umbrella of the Herald group, overseen by Magnus Llewellin. As we have already seen, Llewellin puts financial considerations above all else.

Further proof, if any were needed, that the so-called Nationalist press is running scared, came when a cartoon of Greg Moodie's was not published in the National. As Wings Over Scotland points out, nobody knows what the content was or who might have been offended so no possible litigation was involved. Essentially, the paper was too frightened to run with it.[25]

This immediately begs the question as to what, exactly, the point is of the Sunday Herald claiming to support Scottish independence, or the very existence of the National. It could be argued that giving a voice to those that want Scottish independence is better than nothing; but if that voice is restricted due to fear, then is it really a voice at all?

The sceptical view of these newspapers would be to see them as just a cynical exploitation of a niche market; after all, money seems to be the paramount consideration. The Herald's circulation had been nosediving for years so it is possible that the launch of the National was merely a manoeuvre to get a larger readership. Whatever the truth is, it is obvious that no newspaper can be trusted. All we have is online media and, hopefully, they do not end up succumbing to the pressure of mega-rich Unionists.

Some social media, however, already seem to be undermining the Scottish Government, albeit unconsciously. The support for an opposition, which is in favour of Scottish independence, to the SNP is already evident on some online media. It might seem more democratic, but is this split in the independence vote a good thing?

6
Power To The People!

Mention the People's Front of Judaea and everyone will chuckle, knowing exactly what the joke is. The term is usually applied to small, powerless, left-wing political parties, who have pretensions far beyond their capabilities or support. It was a clever, and funny, part of 'Life of Brian' since it was something that just about everyone would recognise. The wee man, sitting on his own, who constituted the total membership of the Judaean People's Front, was something else that most of us recognised immediately.

The best places to encounter these little organisations are at colleges and universities, at trades union conferences and at meetings and demonstrations against poverty, nuclear weapons or wars. You can spot their members easily enough; they are the ones that shout the loudest and they even use megaphones at marches to attempt to drown out everybody else.

My own experience with these characters came about at university, where they would spend ages at Students Union meetings arguing with other small parties. I accompanied friends to some of the party meetings, where, just as in 'Life of Brian', they would debate and argue over resolutions that were never going to become a reality. My abiding memory of all these Wolfie Smiths was that they were unswerving in their belief that they were right and everybody else was wrong and they all appeared to be from comfortable, middle-class backgrounds.

Most of these individuals got their information about

working-class people from the television, which led to some pretty weird misconceptions. I come from Castlemilk, on the south side of Glasgow, which is right on the outskirts and, in the 1970s and 1980s, was right next to dairy and arable farms. (I have not been there for a while so this might well still be the case.) A few of us in our Hall of Residence kitchen at Stirling were talking about wildlife we had encountered and I told of how I came across a fox when emptying the bin one night. This provoked laughter from a Wolfie Smith, who was convinced that Castlemilk was an inner-city area. From what he had seen on the news and current-affairs programmes, working-class folk throughout the UK lived in the inner city. The fact that this individual actually came from Glasgow made his ignorance ten times worse!

It is hard to discern what makes these characters join left-wing parties; I always assumed that it was some kind of social guilt that inspired them. As I said earlier, they all seemed to be middle-class and were all convinced that they knew what was best for their poor, downtrodden inferiors. The ungrateful, working-class wretches, however, refused to rally to the cause; not that this deterred our Wolfie Smiths. In their minds, the working classes merely needed to waken up, tear themselves away from their televisions, football, pop music and pubs and they would see the truth and throw off their shackles.

Out in the real world, many of these characters abandon their youthful politics later in life but there are some that cling on, determined that ordinary people need to be saved from themselves. Sometimes they have a bit of success, as the Scottish Socialist Party did in the early 21st Century, only for internal arguments to bring everything crashing down.

It perhaps seems unfair to label all these parties as middle-class; after all, Tommy Sheridan and Rosie Kane were from working-class backgrounds. The truth is, though, that much of the influence on these parties is middle-class and most of the senior members have been to university. This last point might seem petty but it does make a difference.

It does not matter how many marches you go on, how much you support strikes or even how long you have been on the dole; the fact is, that if you have been to university, then you do not have the same life experience as other working-class people. You have more opportunities than those folk will ever have and it is mostly up to you whether or not you take them. You can move, or even go abroad, and work as a teacher or whatever; those other people cannot. You are not one of them, no matter how much you try to convince yourself, and others, that you are.

In Castlemilk there used to be student accommodation in the Mitchelhill Flats. A bus was laid on to take the students straight from these high-rise flats to their places of study and back. Essentially, these students might have been resident in Castlemilk but they did not *live* there. They had very little, or no, interaction with other residents and were in no way a part of life in Castlemilk. That, however, did not stop some of them claiming, for political ends, that they knew what it was like to live in a deprived area. It was all reminiscent of the Pulp song, 'Common People'.

To get back to our People's-Front-of-Judaea parties, many of them were prominent in the campaign for Scottish independence during the Referendum. This helped to bring them a popularity that some of them had never experienced before. It must have been a heady experience for them and they looked to capitalise on it.

Knowing that they had no chance on their own, these small organisations decided to band together and campaign for election to the Scottish Parliament as RISE, which stands for Respect, Independence, Socialism and Environmentalism.[1] Colin Fox, national co-spokesman of the Scottish Socialist Party, said, 'We want to make it absolutely clear that the independence movement does not belong to the SNP, it is not Nicola's plaything.'[2]

That sounded unnecessarily bellicose, but one of the comments on the story was, perhaps, much more telling. It simply said, 'Anyone but SNP.'[3] Was this coalition going to provide a conduit for anti-SNP voters, who knew that their own parties had no chance of success?

Unionist newspapers were quick to announce the organisation's birth, the Daily Record's headline saying, 'New left-wing coalition RISE vow to become main opposition to

SNP at Holyrood'.[4] That, however, was not what the Unionist press was looking for. Not everyone in Scotland was going to vote SNP in the Holyrood elections and it was to be expected that there would still be Labour, Liberal-Democrat and Conservative MSPs to provide opposition to the Scottish Government. What the Unionist media really saw in this new political organisation was an opportunity to split the Scottish independence vote, with the hope that less SNP members would be elected.

RISE was not like the SDP in the 1980s, which, in its early stages at least, had many members and seemed to be providing something new. RISE, in contrast, was a pretty small-scale affair; only 450 people turned up to its launch, which was reduced to 200 by the end of the day.[5] This new Socialist alliance seemed to be getting far more media attention than its numbers warranted, which immediately made one suspicious about the agenda of those media.

A perusal of the people standing as list candidates showed that it was full of middle-class professionals and well-known politicians.[6] As one Socialist, not affiliated to RISE, pointed out:

> I'm not actually sure how many ordinary working people there are on the RISE candidates list rather than folks who are already working in journalism or politics, or folks who are journalism and politics graduates.[7]

It was hardly what one would call a 'grass-roots' movement. It seemed to be another parade of Trotskyists that knew what was best for the proletariat. The Daily Record had an article, in which two RISE list candidates told how 'working on the frontline of Scotland's services has encouraged them to stand for change.'[8] Not *living*, you will notice, but *working*.

Looking at some of the leading lights in RISE was instructive too. Cat Boyd is the daughter of two teachers (her mother was a head teacher and is now a heid-bummer in education) and studied International Politics at Strathclyde University. She has been a trade-unionist and left-wing political activist for years now.[9] Apart from that information it is difficult to find anything else about her. Where did she grow up, what school did she go to, what job did she have that got her into a trade union? This mystery is no doubt deliberate. It is not your fault if you grow up in a middle-class area and went to a posh school, but it does not help if you want to play the working-class hero, as Boyd frequently does.

Another major player in RISE is novelist and playwright Alan Bissett,[10] while Mike Small, who runs the website Bella Caledonia, is described as an activist, author and publisher.[11] Neither of this pair could exactly be described as blue-collar workers. Their colleague, Jonathon Shafi, is another one with a mysterious background. He seems to have been mostly, like Boyd, working as some kind of professional activist.

It could, of course, be argued that this is being completely unfair. One could equally point at SNP candidates, or those of other parties for that matter, and say how middle-class or well-off they are. Our media did just that when the papers went overboard about the price of Nicola Sturgeon's coffee machine.[12] The SNP, however, was not claiming to be a grass-roots, working-class organisation; unlike RISE.[13]

Another important point is the internecine feuds that constantly plague small, Socialist parties. We have already seen how other parties can have this problem; notably the SNP in Coatbridge, but Socialism seems to bring out the worst in people. The particular problem for Socialism is that they have their own versions of the Bible and, just like in the days of the Reformation, different readings produce different conclusions with often disastrous results. Marx, Engels, Lenin, Trotsky and others too numerous to mention provide a blueprint for Socialism; unfortunately, all of these writers are open to interpretation and not everyone agrees about what Socialism actually entails or how to go about achieving it.

The cracks in RISE were evident even before the organisation was up and running. One of the main points raised at the launch was that Tommy Sheridan should be excluded. There is no point in going over all the business of Sheridan's trials; suffice it to say that he is seen as somebody that would put voters off. As Colin Fox, a spokesperson for

RISE put it, 'It's part of RISE's attraction that he's not part of it.'[14] They certainly do not believe in 'forgive and forget' in Socialist circles!

The unwillingness to include Sheridan was, perhaps, understandable but the vindictiveness did not end there. Patricia Smith was listed as a RISE candidate for the Lothians but members of RISE, on seeing her name, called for her removal. She was forced to resign and her name disappeared from the list. Her crime? She spoke as a defence witness at Tommy Sheridan's trials.[15]

Meanwhile, not all Socialists have rallied to the RISE banner. Socialist Party Scotland, which is totally distinct from the Scottish Socialist Party (yes, I know), took part in the launch event for RISE, but refused to join. Philip Stott of the SPS was actually pretty scathing about the whole thing, pointing out the lack of a coherent policy and questioning the Socialist credentials of RISE.[16] It made one wonder how long this alliance could last.

No matter what you say about these Socialists, and no matter how hard it is for them to get on with each other, there is no denying their sincerity. They actually want to make life better for a lot of people and you cannot fault them for that. What one could fault them on was the timing of this electoral campaign. There was something about it that smacked of cynicism.

Left-wing organisations have a long history of being infiltrated. Back in the 1980s the papers used to be full of stories about Militant, CND, trades unions and any, even remotely, left-wing body being run from Moscow. Whether this was true or not, and there probably were Soviet plants here and there, far more sinister was the infiltration of these groups by the police. In the climate of the time, where being 'politically active' was almost considered a crime in itself, these undercover police officers were there for purely political reasons.[17]

There had long been links between the police and the Economic League[18] and anyone that ended up on the League's notorious list soon found himself having extreme difficulty securing employment. The League's power was curtailed in the 1990s but it is well known that blacklists still circulate, especially in the construction industry.[19] That, however, was not the limit of what police spies got up to.

It seems that police spies were working high up in left-wing organisations and attempted to have an influence on policy and methods. For example, the police officer that infiltrated Youth Against Racism in Europe in the 1990s was apparently against the peaceful methods of the group. He argued constantly for going out and fighting the BNP on the streets. Those are not the actions of a spy; they are the actions of an agent provocateur.[20]

Whenever there have been political demonstrations, especially in London and even in recent years, there is an element that mixes in with the genuine protesters, faces covered with masks or scarves, which goes out of its way to start trouble, often leading to running battles with the police and looting.[21] These people are described as agenda-driven anarchists or just common criminals, looking to take advantage of situations.

There is a third possibility when seeking to explain who these itinerant troublemakers are, one that the media, of course, shies away from; they could well be police agents provocateurs. It is not as if the police have not done such things before. The obvious question, though, is what do the police hope to achieve with such tactics? The answer is obvious; it is to undermine left-wing organisations and destroy their reputations in the eyes of the general public.

This kind of thing is not unusual. Adolf Hitler, for example, was a spy for the German army, who infiltrated the NSDAP and ended up taking it over, changing it from a workers' party to one endorsed by big business and the military. In our own country suspicions are growing that the IRA bombing campaign was actually orchestrated by MI5 in order to discredit Irish Republicanism.[22] (I used this premise myself as a plot device in my novel, 'Catalyst' – shameless plug!) It is more than likely that such tactics are common; after all, the CIA is well-known for interfering in politics in other countries.

Of course, this possibility occurred to the supporters of RISE as well and they were proactive in denying and ridiculing such accusations before they appeared. Angela

Haggerty in the Sunday Herald, not long before she was sacked, joked that she would be accused of 'secretly working for MI5'.[23] If, however, MI5 was doing its job properly, Ms Haggerty would be completely unaware that she was doing its bidding.

Putting aside this theory that RISE was in the pocket of the Establishment, there was another aspect of the organisation to consider. Socialism is an internationalist political cause, following the precepts set down by Trotsky. One only has to look at the Soviet Union to see how a Socialist economy in a capitalist world is doomed to failure. Trotskyists have long seen nationalism as a Stalinist pursuit; something to be avoided at all costs.[24] In fact, the only ones to get involved with nationalists are Stalinist traitors to the working class.[25]

This, obviously, put RISE in an awkward position. Should they put their nationalism first, or their socialism? It was all very well getting the support of online media, like Common Space and Bella Caledonia but, if they really wanted votes, the support of the mainstream media was their best bet. And it looked as if they had decided to go for it.

On 9th February 2016, a private-member's bill was put forward in the Scottish Parliament. This bill was about changing the current opt-in way of donating organs to an opt-out method and was being put forward by Labour MSP, Anne McTaggart. All parties left it as a free vote; all, that is, except for Labour, who, inexplicably, decided to use the whip and make it a party issue.[26]

The proposal was defeated, with a Government amendment to agree to the proposal's merit but to undertake a consultation to address serious concerns and to look at how the opt-out method worked in Wales being passed.[27] Probably with tongue firmly in cheek, SNP MSP John Mason suggested on Twitter that it was the decision to have Jackie Baillie close the debate that had put some SNP members off voting for McTaggart's bill.[28]

Mason accused Baillie of being overly party-political[29] and one can just imagine her, fingers jabbing the air, blaming the SNP for everything. It was ridiculous, however, to suggest that her speech was the main reason for the bill's failure. In fact, there were genuine concerns about the soft opt-out scheme, not least of which was the delay that could possibly be involved in finding family members to get permission to remove organs from the deceased.[30] Our media, though, decided to run with John Mason's tweet; it fitted well with their anti-SNP agenda.

The Daily Record was quick off the mark as usual and decided to tug at the readers' heartstrings by printing a piece written by a man whose wife suffers from cystic fibrosis; a condition which might mean the need for a lung transplant sometime in the future.[31] The whole article was all about blaming the SNP, claiming that people were going to die while the Scottish Government played party politics. It was a pretty damning tirade.

One conclusion that could be drawn from the piece is that the author was a member of Scottish Labour, looking to turn everyone against the SNP Government. There was no need, however, to rush to Google to find out; the Record, at the end of the article, provided the answer.[32] The writer of the article was actually a contributor to Angela Haggerty's Common Space website and was standing for election to Holyrood as a RISE candidate.

It looked as if the strategy that RISE was going to use in the coming election had emerged; they were going to try to step into the shoes vacated by Scottish Labour. In fact, Cat Boyd had said as much in September 2015.[33] It seemed also as if the Daily Record, and possibly other parts of the media, were only too keen to help. To repeat a comment that appeared on the story of the launch of RISE, 'Anyone but SNP.'[34] Our media were obviously taking that particular call to arms seriously. In fact, Daily Record writer, Gerry Hassan, on 13th March 2016, was calling for 'more radical and outspoken voices in our parliament.'[35] It hardly takes a genius to work out who his talking about.

The two main supporters of RISE appeared to be the website Bella Caledonia, which had prominent RISE member, Cat Boyd, as a regular contributor[36] and Common Space. Both sites seemed to think there was something sinister about asking parties, supposedly in favour of independence, to wait until we get independence before looking to get elected; 'Wheesht for indy', as Angela Haggerty called it.[37] This point of view, however, denied the fact that it was everyone pulling together that led to 45% of the electorate voting for independence in the Referendum. Believing that splitting up and sniping at each other was somehow going to increase that vote betrays a remarkable naivety.

In 1848 the opportunity for Germany to unite as a proper federal state, instead of coming under the sway of the militarism of Prussia, was lost due to bickering at the assembly. In Northern Ireland, Irish Republican Nationalism has not gained the mass support that it could have done, in part due to the wide array of Republican organisations that the people have been faced with over the years: the IRA, the Provisional IRA, the Real IRA, Continuity IRA, the INLA and God knows what else. Having different organisations, ostensibly working toward the same end, constantly sniping at each other is manifestly counter-productive.

So why would websites that claim to want Scottish independence throw their support behind an organisation that was going to undermine the whole campaign? Naivety, rather than cynicism, seemed to be the answer, though only the people that run these websites could really tell us. One thing that is worth pointing out, however, is that it was not only through supporting RISE that Bella Caledonia was undermining the cause of Scottish independence. That is the subject of the next chapter.

7
The Makar's New Clothes

One of the constant criticisms levelled at the SNP and, by extension, the whole independence movement during the Referendum was that it was backward-looking. Tartan, clans and shortbread were the SNP's calling cards, while celebrating the Battle of Bannockburn was an attempt to tap into some kind of atavistic impulse.[1] Some commentators even equated the SNP's appeal with the Nazi's use of 'national spirit' in the 1930s.[2]

The truth was that this was a lot of utter nonsense. The only past that the SNP, and others involved in the Independence Referendum, called up was to do with how Scotland had been lied to and swindled by Westminster in the past few decades. Neither was there a call for an insular, inward-looking Scotland; the intention was for the country to stay in the EU, unlike many in the Unionist parties.

Anyone that knows me will know that one of my pet hates is when people try to promote 'Scots' as our true language. Some kind of myth has grown that this language was beaten out of us and replaced with English. Liz Lochhead promotes this theory in her poem 'Kidspoem/Bairnsang', with the idea that you had to speak and write a certain way at school; 'as if you were posh, grown-up, male, English and dead'.[3] The truth, though, is rather different.

Schools in Scotland were not like those in South Africa, where Boer children were often sent to the dunce's corner, wearing a sign saying, 'I am a donkey. I speak Afrikaans.'

There was a concerted effort there to wipe out the Boers' language; there was no such organised campaign in Scotland. At school in Scotland you learned standardised English, as you also had to do if you lived in Newcastle, Manchester or even London. The way you spoke with your friends and family was fine but you also had to be able to converse with people from other areas, or even from abroad. This is called progress, rather than an attempt at linguistic domination.

Nobody in Britain uses Standard English in everyday speech; it is purely there to be employed, both in speaking and writing, as a tool for understanding between people of different places. In a way it is like Esperanto, an invented, common language that we can all share, while using our own language when at home. But the myth that teachers were employed to beat our way of talking out of us has taken root and has made many people have a hatred for Standard English that is completely irrational.

My father-in-law was one of these and refused to converse in anything other than his native, Midlothian way of speaking. He came on holiday with us to Tenerife and discovered, on the first day, that he had forgotten to bring his heart tablets with him. He made an appointment with a local doctor and asked me to come with him in case her English was not that great and I could attempt to explain in my school Spanish. The poor doctor's jaw hit the floor when she was bombarded with the following:

Ah goat tayblits fur ma hert aff the lady doactur in Bonnyrigg, but Ah've left thum in the hoose. Ah need tae take thum, ken, ur ma hert wulnae work right!

Of course, rather than translating into Spanish, I had to translate this into English before he could get his prescription.

This situation sums up succinctly why it is necessary to know Standard English. Most people in Scotland have realised this for well over a century and even Gaelic speakers insisted on their children learning English so that they could get on in life, even if this meant sending them away from home to schools on the mainland.

To suggest that 'Scots' was banned from the classroom would be to ignore the experience of practically every schoolchild in Scotland. It was in January every year that the mutterings of 'Aw, naw!' could be heard all over the country as the teacher passed round tattered copies of the poems of Robert Burns. Nobody liked them and nobody understood them but you were forced to learn them because that was Scotland's National Bard, writing in 'your' language.

And therein lies the real problem with 'Scots' in our schools. It had nothing whatsoever to do with replacing our spoken language with English and everything to do with our spoken language not being considered proper 'Scots' at all. Burns's 'Scots' was the real language, while what you spoke was but a second-rate dialect of English.

The language spoken by English people, of whatever dialect, is nothing like that spoken by their ancestors two hundred years ago. Equally in Scotland nobody speaks like Burns anymore, apart from those that go out of their way to do so. There always seems to be a parade of these folk on the TV, usually wee men with long hair and beards, who are all 'unco' this' and 'unco' that'. None of us has a clue what they are babbling on about. But they are supposedly speaking real 'Scots'.

There is a publishing imprint called Itchy Coo, which strives to bring the 'Scots language' into schools and homes. Part of this involves translating well-known books into 'Scots'.[4] Hand any Scottish child a 'Scots' translation of Roald Dahl's 'Fantastic Mr Fox'[5] and their first reaction will be, 'What the hell's a tod?' As one (positive) commenter says on Amazon:

> A great way to encourage the next generation to appreciate and understand the Scots language. Reading a familiar popular story helps to break the barrier of unknown words and should help maintain interest in Scots language and culture.[6]

Is the idea, then, that children have to unlearn their spoken Scots and replace it with this ancient language? When I first started teaching in East Lothian I found it funny that the children called a banana a 'bananny'. They, in turn, found it hilarious that I found what was, to them, an everyday word funny. Parents used to joke that you could always tell when a child had been in Mr Anderson's class since they would come home talking about 'weans' instead of 'bairns'! Are we to get rid of this diversity of language and all talk of 'puddocks, gowks and bubblyjocks' from the Shetlands to the Borders?

It rather defeats the purpose when children are to be told that the language they speak is not proper Scots and that they have to learn the *real* Scots at school. No doubt the good 'fowk' at Itchy Coo, and other enthusiasts for 'Scots' would argue that this is not the case at all. But if they are trying to promote the idea of children cherishing their own language, then why introduce these Rabbie-Burns-lingo books, to read which the children will need recourse to a glossary?

Essentially, what is being disseminated is the idea that the language that Scottish children speak is somehow inferior and second-class. These middle-class scholars are going to teach the children how they should be speaking. Is this not the attitude that they are supposed to be getting rid of?

Bella Caledonia, it seems, supports this idea of getting everyone to speak 'Scots'.[7] One of the comments on the site quotes someone on a website about Robert Burns, who said that the Scots language was killed off by a 'self-appointed intelligentsia'.[8] This is ironic since it is a 'self-appointed intelligentsia' that now wants us all to go around speaking a language from two-hundred-odd years ago.

Looking at the contributors to Bella Caledonia, flicking through the contents and reading the articles is a bit like watching one of those late-night review programmes you get on BBC2. You know the kind of thing, full of folk for whom Socialism means more money for the performing arts and a presenter that is fond of saying, 'If I could turn to you…'. The whole site appears to be filled with middle-class, arty-farty types; just the sort that promote the use of 'Scots' in our schools.

One major point of interest on this website is the appointment of a new *Makar*, a sort of Scottish version of the Poet Laureate. Since 2011 this post has been taken by Liz Lochhead and before her by Edwin Morgan; both darlings of Scotland's self-appointed intelligentsia. Names are put forward for a new *Makar* on Bella Caledonia; names with which the majority of us will be unfamiliar. A bit of snobbery shows its ugly head. As the writer of the piece points out, the *Makar* is chosen by a panel of the current, and previous First Ministers. He goes on, 'Could anyone imagine Cameron, Blair and Major sitting down to discuss the next Poet Laureate? Pam Ayres anyone?'[9]

Unfortunately for this pathetic put-down, people of a certain age in Scotland are probably far more familiar with the poems of Pam Ayres, and would enjoy them more, than those of anyone being considered for the post of *Makar*. Even in one of the comments the suggestion that we all vote for the *Makar* is tempered with the caveat that we would choose from a selection put forward by experts.[10] God forbid that we should actually choose somebody *popular*!

The fact is that if the Scottish people were to vote for their favourite poem, Duncan MacRae's 'Wee Cock Sparra'[11] would come out well ahead of anything by Hugh McDiarmid.[12] Our self-appointed intelligentsia probably has a collective breakdown just thinking about that. Anything popular, or, as they would term it, 'populist', is immediately dismissed as of no relevance by these folk; unless, of course, it happens to be a couple of centuries old.

This Scottish intelligentsia is self-perpetuating, allowing only certain new people into its hallowed ranks. A *sine qua non* for membership seems to be thinking of Alasdair Gray's 'Lanark' as the greatest piece of writing since the dawn of mankind, sacred texts included. Mention 'No Mean City' in these folk's midst and you will be burned at the stake. Meanwhile, Burns is held as the acme of Scottish poetry, as well as a template for the Scots language.

It is quite ironic how, on the one hand, these people decry our education system for, allegedly, trying to make us all conform to a uniform way of speaking and writing and yet, on the other, present us with a *de facto*, standardised version of our own language.

Perhaps they envision a Scottish version of *L'Académie*

Française,[13] a rather ridiculous institution that fights a failing battle against 'Franglais', the use of English terms in French language. Words like *le weekend*, *le sandwich*, *l'email* and *le football* are anathema to this elitist group, which hardly seems to live in the real world at all. The current hegemony of American culture in music and cinema has given it plenty to have apoplexy about over the past number of years. Ordinary French people, however, ignore the edicts of this old-fashioned institution.

Our Scottish Academy, however, could be made of sterner stuff and Itchy Coo has already provided some standard texts for the teaching of 'proper' language. Perhaps we shall see a time when primary-school children, rather than the myth of getting into trouble for saying 'puddock' instead of 'frog', will get into trouble for *not* saying 'puddock'!

Of course, the denizens of Bella Caledonia would dispute all this and there is a video on the website with a woman speaking about ordinary, everyday language.[14] Unfortunately, she tries to perpetuate the myth that our everyday language was somehow undermined by being taught Standard English. The comments below the video also rather contradict the message that the language we all speak in our everyday lives is what is being promoted.

One commenter speaks of his local MP as being for 'Glesgae North East'. Who in Glasgow ever calls it 'Glesgae'? Or how about this one: 'Canna agree wi her anent authenticity – it's an undeemous-lik bruckle a threip.' Or this: 'Aw the bairns in oor faimly hae mithers/faithers grannies an grandas wha aw speik Scots amang oorsels yit nane o thir bairns speik it e'n whan they're no at the schuil.' Or this one: 'Scots is haud bak bi such fowk, intentionally sae.'[15] Does anybody actually speak like that and, more to the point, does anybody understand it?

One individual suggests having 'a Scots Language TV Station' and 'a Scots Language 'National Certificate'' Both these suggestions, however, present obvious problems. Shove a Glaswegian and an Aberdonian in the same room and get them to converse with each other in their everyday language. It would soon be discovered that neither of them had the first idea of what the other was talking about. So in which everyday language would a Scots language TV station and a Scots language National Certificate be presented? The only answer would be to teach Standard Scots in schools in exactly the same way as Standard English is taught. Effectively, you would be telling children that the language they speak is inferior and not 'proper' Scots.

And so we are back to where we came in. A self-appointed, linguistic elite would determine what is 'Scots' and what is not. And what will constitute this 'Proper Scots'? As we have seen, that has already been decided. We are to start learning and speaking as Robert Burns wrote two-hundred years ago.

So how does this nonsense impact on the Scottish Government? Well, since the website promoting this stuff also purports to support Scottish independence, it is fairly obvious that a link will be established in people's minds. Scottish independence, the inference could easily be, will lead to some kind of linguistic fascism, where we are all forced to speak as they did in Robert Burns's time. Perhaps we might even have the equivalent of Karen Dunbar's 'Cliché Cops' arresting us if we stray from the path of 'proper' Scots language.

Mention Scottish independence to most people and they will immediately think of the SNP. All those tiny, Socialist parties would not even occur to them, even if they had heard of RISE. So all this snooty rubbish about *makars*, what we should be reading and how we should be speaking would be blamed on the SNP.

It sounds ridiculous but it certainly fits in with the notion that the SNP is a backward-looking party. Folk like George Foulkes would jump at the chance of highlighting the promotion of an obsolete language as concrete proof that the SNP want to take us back to some far-off time in the past, when we ate heather and thistles and women looked after the 'bairns' while their men tossed their cabers all day long. I doubt that George Foulkes and his ilk read Bella Caledonia but somebody would be bound to point it out to them if it looked as if Scottish independence were to become a reality.

One wonders if the SNP is aware of this and is, perhaps, taking measures to counter this association of them with a dead language that nobody speaks. A website had apparently been set up by the Scottish Government to 'celebrate' the Scots language. It was soon discovered by experts that some of the words made no sense at all. 'Gobbledygook,' they called it.[16]

The Scottish Government apologised and fixed the mistakes.[17] That the errors were made in the first place, however, shows the Scottish Government in a positive light. It proves that nobody really uses this language, making errors inevitable. That it took 'experts' to notice the mistakes points up another issue that is quite encouraging; the SNP Government cares about the resurrection of this dead language as little as the rest of us do! Still, that will not stop our pompous, pretentious, self-elected intelligentsia from continuing to promote it.

Rather unconsciously, then, the likes of Bella Caledonia are doing a disservice to the SNP-led Scottish Government. Not unconscious at all, however, are the attempts by our mainstream media to forge negative links to the SNP in our minds. That is what we are going to look at next.

8
The Sneaky Stuff

During the Scottish Independence Referendum campaign our media did their utmost to avoid looking at the issues altogether. Instead, they tried to pursue a policy of smear against the SNP, ignoring the fact that others were involved in campaigning for independence. The same tactics were employed in the General Election of 2015 and, since neither they, nor the Labour Party they supported, had anything else to offer, they continued to smear the SNP and its members relentlessly.

We have already seen how our press was ready to blame the Scottish Government for everything; even taking the side of the Tories to pursue their agenda. Personal attacks were employed as well; anything to get us to see the SNP in a bad light. A third way was used too; one that needed a subtler approach.

Homelessness is a topic that deserves as much publicity as possible. There are people sleeping rough out there, through no fault of their own. Many of them suffer from serious psychological problems and include a lot of ex-soldiers, flung on the scrapheap when they are no longer useful. The Daily Record highlighted the problem in February 2016, printing a story about a young man, suffering from depression, who was living in a tent in Edinburgh's New Town. Unfortunately, that was not all the Record had to say.

The headline screamed a massive implication that would not be lost on anyone:

> Homeless man who suffers from depression sleeping in tent just 300 yards from Nicola Sturgeon's front door.[1]

There was no question about what we were meant to glean from that! The article went on to tell about what the poor man had gone through; the headline, however, would make sure that it was not him that would be uppermost in people's minds.

The man himself said that 'staying 300 yards from Bute House wasn't a political statement. It was just a sheltered spot to avoid the worst of the weather.' The Record, though, made sure that its main point was rammed home by pointing out that the young man was 'pitched up in a street behind Edinburgh's Charlotte Square, home to Bute House and properties worth millions.'

It was obvious what inference we were meant to make; selfish millionaire, Nicola Sturgeon, had the homeless living practically on her doorstep but was doing nothing about it. It is the headline that gives the game away.

The Record has a habit of having headlines that bear little relevance to the actual story. For example, football managers are said to be 'raging' when they have merely expressed 'concern'. This is bad enough but, often, the headlines betray a rather shameful agenda.

> Scots mum waiting for double hand transplant welcomes NHS decision to offer procedure in England

was one such headline at the end of January 2016.[2] The obvious conclusion to be drawn from that was that the woman was unable to get the operation done in Scotland and was having to have it done in England. A cursory read of the article showed that the woman lost her hands due to septicaemia and had been waiting for a transplant for eighteen months.

A closer read of the piece, however, reveals that this remarkably brave individual was not moaning or blaming anybody for her situation. In fact, all she was doing was highlighting the plight of all those awaiting transplants in general and was calling for more people to sign up as donors.

And as for England doing hand transplants, the woman was praising them for following the example of the NHS in Scotland, where the procedure had already been available for years.

And it was not just the Daily Record that was at this quasi-subliminal approach. Have a look at this headline in the Scotsman: 'Ministers accused of cover-up over historic sexual abuse'.[3] That, of course, conjures up pictures of the Elm Guest House, paedophile rings at Westminster and the scandal over supposedly missing documents. Surely the Scottish Government was not involved in this sordid business as well? It most emphatically was not, as the article made clear.

The Scottish Government had announced in 2014 that it was going to institute an enquiry into the historic abuse of children in care.[4] Everybody welcomed this but, during 2015 and into 2016, there were demands for the enquiry to widen its scope. What about the Catholic Church, voluntary organisations, like the Boy Scouts or even ordinary dayschools?[5] There were even calls for an investigation into the so-called 'Magic Circle', an alleged organised paedophile ring at the top of Scottish society.[6] The organisations calling for the enquiry's scope to be extended accused the Scottish Government of effectively covering up for those outside the investigation's remit; hence the Scotsman's headline.

It was difficult to understand what the extension of the enquiry would achieve, other than to expose the perpetrators and perhaps lead to them being prosecuted. Not that this would be a bad thing; on the contrary, it is something that should, indeed, must be done. Whether the Government is the right body to deal with this, however, is another matter entirely.

Police Scotland set up its National Child Abuse Investigation Unit in 2014 and it is this body that should be looking into the 'Magic Circle' etc. The unit's remit is to combat organised child abuse, which is what those decrying the Scottish Government's enquiry want. It is to the police that those wanting child-abuse gangs investigated should be speaking, not Holyrood.

As for the Scottish Government's enquiry itself, the idea is to look at what happened in care homes, residential schools and the like; institutions which the Scottish Government, and the Scottish Office before it, was responsible for. The Government wanted to ensure that safeguards were put in place so that such things never happened again. The remit of the enquiry was to identify past mistakes so that they were never repeated; not to name, shame and prosecute. Our media, of course, understands this fully but they are never ones to pass up an opportunity to have a dig at the SNP, no matter how low they have to stoop in the process. Even helping to stir up sectarianism was not beneath them.

Lanarkshire, North and South, is very often in the news for all the wrong reasons. Sectarianism seems to be a bigger problem there than anywhere else in Scotland; certainly bigger than in Glasgow. In North Lanarkshire there is the predominantly Catholic Coatbridge and the mostly Protestant Airdrie, while in South Lanarkshire is the infamous Larkhall.[7] In the early 21st Century, North Lanarkshire Council was the leader in promoting writing in schools. Other councils used its writing scheme successfully; this, however, never made it into the papers. It seems that only sectarianism makes the news, which is unfair since the majority of people in the two council areas probably could not care less about religion.

Sectarianism was prominent in the 1994 by-election in East Monklands, one of the two constituencies in the area at that time. For years there had been complaints that the council was being run by a Catholic clique and that money was being spent on Catholic areas, like Coatbridge, while Protestant areas, like Airdrie, were largely ignored. There were also stories about separate application forms for council jobs, favouring Catholics over Protestants. Much was made of the fact that the leading Labour Party on the council was entirely composed of Roman Catholics. 'Monklandsgate', as this purported scandal was named, was given a veneer of veracity when Professor Robert Black's report into the affair confirmed that all the rumours were true.[8]

Black's report was brandished in the House of Commons by John Major and formed a large part of the Tories' campaign in the by-election. The Labour candidate, Helen

Liddell, was quick to attack the councillors of her own party.[9] She also decided to play her own 'Orange card' by blaming the monks of Buckfast Abbey for all the social evils in the area.[10]

A proper investigation, by William Nimmo Smith QC, found that the council had no case to answer.[11] That, however, did not make sectarianism go away and it bubbles away in the background to this day. FOI requests are made for blatantly sectarian reasons; for example, asking how much St. Patrick's Day festivities cost the council while ignoring the annual cost of Orange parades in the area.[12]

The Labour Party in the whole of Lanarkshire has been affected by 'Monklandsgate' and, ever since, has tended to stray onto the Orange side of sectarian issues. For example, a Labour MSP actually supported what was effectively vandalism on council property in 2001.[13] Meanwhile, the Labour Party in Scotland continued to target Buckfast tonic wine as the sole reason for anti-social behaviour.[14]

2016 saw the centenary of the Easter Rising in Dublin. Plans had already been drawn up to commemorate the event in Ireland and throughout the world, wherever there were people of Irish descent. North Lanarkshire Council, where many Irish immigrants settled, was approached and asked to fly the flag of the Irish Republic on its buildings as a commemoration. The matter came before the corporate services committee, which narrowly passed the proposal.[15]

It would not be the first time that a Scottish council had flown a foreign flag; West Dunbartonshire Council had, a couple of years previously, flown the Palestinian flag on its building to support the people suffering in Gaza.[16] Flying the Irish flag, however, was a different matter entirely; there were people out there just waiting to be offended.

An organisation called Regimental Blues decided that it was appropriate to publish on its website details of all those on the corporate services committee that had voted in favour of the flag being flown. These details included addresses, telephone numbers and even mobile numbers with the suggestion that readers of the site should 'Please feel free to use these details for objection purposes!' A message was sent to the council, full of thinly-veiled threats and ending with the warning, 'We will be watching. We have the winning hand here and we strongly suggest you do not call our bluff.'[17]

It could, of course, be argued that the decision to fly this flag was being unnecessarily provocative, especially in a place like North Lanarkshire. That, however, does not excuse the bigotry of Regimental Blues, which has a history of anti-Irish racism. It is, perhaps, ironic that cities and towns in England, which bore the brunt of the IRA bombing campaign, can easily distinguish between the IRA, the Irish Republic and Irish people. Meanwhile there are people in Scotland, which was untouched by the IRA, who tend to lump the IRA, Ireland, Irish people, folk of Irish descent, Catholicism and even Glasgow Celtic into one, homogeneous mass. While the rest of the world enjoyed St Patrick's Day in 2015, the only sign of a celebration in Glasgow was Regimental Blues trying to stir up trouble in the East End of the city.[18]

As things stood the proposal to fly the Irish flag still had to go before the whole council and it seemed unlikely that it would be passed. Labour promised that, as the controlling group on the council, it would be voting against the proposal. Apparently, this had nothing to do with the Irish flag specifically but the council not wanting to set a precedent and be inundated with requests to fly other flags.[19] The Evening Times also mentioned the threats, though only in passing and it failed to mention Regimental Blues explicitly. A North Lanarkshire paper failed to mention anything about the threats at all; it was more concerned about which party had been responsible for passing the proposal in the first place.

'SNP councillors behind Irish flag vote,' screeched the headline in the Cumbernauld News.[20] In fact, two Labour councillors had voted to pass the proposal as well but that information was hidden away in the article; there was no point spoiling a good headline with the truth. The implication of not mentioning the threats from Regimental Blues was that it appeared that the paper was taking sides in the argument. Apparently, the Irish flag was something evil and the SNP was just as evil for even countenancing flying the thing.

The Daily Record reported that the flag-flying was not

going to happen but it was decided at that paper to try to put a more positive spin on the news. Rather than explicitly blame the SNP for the whole thing, the Record article was all about the Labour Party stepping in to save the day.[21] Like the Cumbernauld News, the Record declined to mention anything about Regimental Blues or its threats. This was rather strange since the paper is usually at pains to tell us that 'one side is as bad as the other' when it comes to sectarian bigotry. Not on this occasion, though. It was all down to those nasty Republicans and their nasty flag, as well as their friends in the SNP.

There was a petition to campaign against the flag being flown, which was signed by more than 1400 people.[22] In a population of well over 300,000 souls[23] this hardly seemed overwhelming. The truth is that the vast majority of people probably could not care less. The council could have flown the Jolly Roger and most folk would neither have noticed nor bothered about it. Bigots are in a minority in Scotland but they tend to make more noise than everyone else.

Whatever the rights and wrongs of the situation our media were obviously clear in their message; they thought the whole idea was a disgrace. And who had brought this disgrace to the doors of North Lanarkshire Council? Why, the SNP, of course. Links between Scottish Nationalism and Irish Republicanism have long been a favoured theme on some of the more insane corners of the internet. Our media had now given this notion credence and possibly placed the connection in minds that, otherwise, would never have believed it.

Sometimes the press did not bother to mention the Scottish Government or the SNP; they no longer needed to. On the 21st February, the Sunday Mail had this headline: 'Revealed: Scots Jail drug busts at all-time high as number of cases treble in five years'.[24] The paper did not have to say that this was the fault of the Scottish Government; we had all been well-trained to know in which direction the hidden finger was pointing.

Just in case some of us were too dumb to make the proper inference, the paper provided its usual introduction, right below the by-line:

Figures obtained by the Sunday Mail show drugs finds by prison officers since 2011 have soared from around 15 a week to more than 40.[25]

Now, what was significant about the year 2011? Why, that was the year when the SNP gained a majority at Holyrood and was the first party in Scotland to be able to run a government on its own!

The article was a pretty damning indictment of a prison service in disarray, though that was not necessarily the case. Tucked away in the middle of the piece was the following information:

The Scottish Prison Service say the increase in seizures is down to more sophisticated security measures, including investment in more staff, drugs detecting equipment and drug dogs.[26]

After this part, which contradicted the paper's agenda, the article changed tack. Scary statistics were given about deadly weapons in prison, along with the news that seizures of such weapons was down. The police, again, attributed this to better methods of detection. Possibly, the police were intervening before any deadly weapons were made or smuggled in. That, however, was not the conclusion the Sunday Mail wanted us to reach. The word 'but' at the beginning of the sentence about the reduction in weapons seizures betrayed what the paper was implying.

So, on the one hand, an increase in drugs seizures was meant to show the failings in the prison service, while, on the other, a decrease in weapons seizures was supposed to show exactly the same thing. It was symptomatic of the desperation of the Scottish press to print anything to the detriment of the Scottish Government that a paper would publish two sets of figures, one showing a rise in reports of one crime, the other a fall in reports of another, and claim that both led to the same conclusion.

Less than a week before, the Daily Record had published a shocking article about prostitution in Scotland. It was a story we had heard before; but that made it no less hard-hitting. It was about how young women are kidnapped from their homes in Eastern Europe, raped, abused, forced into becoming drug addicts and kept as slaves to be sold to men for sex.[27]

One of the comments beneath the article was interesting. It said, 'No doubt Sturgeon will blame this on Westminster too. She blames EVERYTHING on Westminster.'[28] Of course, the point this character was making was that Nicola Sturgeon would be trying to shift the blame, implying that it was actually her fault. The paper itself laid no blame at anyone's door, nor did anyone in the Labour Party; not yet, anyway.

MSP Rhoda Grant has a long history of fighting for women's causes, with a special interest in trying to protect workers in the so-called sex industry. In 2012 she tried to introduce a 'Purchase of Sex' bill, which would make purchasing sex, rather than its sale, a criminal offence. By this means she hoped to reduce demand, which would, in turn, reduce the number of women being forced into the sex trade.[29]

Grant's aims were laudable and nobody was going to shed any tears for clients that were arrested; after all, they were hardly showing concern for the women forced into having sex with them. The problem was that such a law would actually cost a fortune to enforce. The police would have to spend long hours in surveillance, not only to catch suspects but to gather evidence to make a cast-iron case. Such laws have been attempted in the U.S. and we have all seen movies where the police have been successfully accused of entrapment.

On top of that, the Scottish Prostitutes Education Project (Scot-Pep) was opposed to the move, fearing that it would drive prostitution even further underground.[30] That would mean that the help currently available to prostitutes, from organisations like Scot-Pep, would be cut off completely. Not surprisingly, Grant's bill got nowhere.

Grant promised that she would try again with her bill and, on 22nd February 2016, the Daily Record announced that she was going to do so that very day.[31] Apparently, she had been spurred into action by the story in the Record seven days previously. Looking at the minutes of the day at the Scottish Parliament it is clear that no such bill was presented. Perhaps the chamber ran out of time. Rhoda Grant maybe needed to have a word with her party colleagues, Jackie Baillie and Neil Findlay, both of whom seem to have pretty much monopolised the day's proceedings.[32]

One wonders, however, why Grant decided to try to re-introduce her bill at the time she did. With every likelihood that the bill would fail again, for exactly the same reasons, the Daily Record could then, like the commenter on its article of 15th February, blame the SNP for the scandal of the sex trade in Scotland. With the Holyrood elections coming up this would be a perfect opportunity to try to turn people away from voting SNP. A quote from Rhoda Grant herself perhaps gave the game away, 'I hope this motion will help support efforts to make this issue a priority for the next Scottish Parliament.'[33] No prizes for guessing what Grant, and the Daily Record for that matter, hoped the composition of the next Parliament was going to be.

The elections to the Scottish Parliament were not the only time we were going to have to cast a vote in 2016. Only a month after the Holyrood elections there was going to be a referendum on whether or not the UK should stay in the EU. So, not only were we to be bombarded with all manner of media garbage against the SNP, we would also have to endure a lot of right-wing rhetoric about British nationalism.

9
Anti-Union Unionists

David Cameron had promised that there would be a referendum on the UK's membership of the European Union and, with UKIP snapping at the Tories' heels, he was going to have to do it before the next general election. He had a comfortable majority in the House of Commons so there was no need to hurry, he had five years in which to hold the referendum. He decided, however, to name June 23rd 2016 as the date on which we would vote to stay in the EU or not.[1]

The elections for the Scottish Parliament were due to take place on May 5th; seven weeks before the European Referendum. It could be argued that this gap gave enough breathing space but that would be a naïve way of looking at it. Not only were the Scottish Parliamentary elections taking place on May 5th; the elections for the London Assembly, the Mayor of London and the Welsh Assembly were all happening on that day as well. It would be an ingenuous soul indeed that believed the campaign for the European Referendum would not start until May 6th. In fact, it was bound, and probably was meant, to have an influence on the May elections.

No sooner was the date for the referendum announced than the campaign started. As in the Scottish Independence Referendum, this one was going to throw together some strange bedfellows. Probably the weirdest was the Ant and Dec of the 'Grassroots Out' campaign, George Galloway and Nigel Farage.[2] It said something about how low Galloway's political stock had fallen that it was Farage who had to do the apologising and explaining about sharing a platform.[3] Certainly, as Farage believed, Galloway would help spread the message among Muslims[4] but the cost could well be the alienation of Tory and UKIP right wingers.[5] There was also a far more obvious, if unspoken, drawback to having Galloway on board.

The flag wavers of UKIP were especially going to appeal to the Loyalist community in Northern Ireland and its supporters in Scotland. Unfortunately for Grassroots Out, George Galloway is anathema to most of these people, because of his views on Ireland.[6] His only saving grace could possibly be that he campaigned for a NO vote in the Scottish Referendum.

Like the NO campaign in the Scottish Referendum, most of the arguments coming from those wanting to leave the EU were highly negative. It was all the usual stuff about 'faceless bureaucrats', being governed by a far-away government and the whole thing being too big and unwieldy. Ironically enough, the same arguments could be levelled at Westminster by those desiring Scottish independence and London is closer to Brussels than it is to anywhere in Scotland. Nobody, however, would be taking any notice of that during this campaign. It was British nationalism that would be to the fore; not Scottish nationalism.

The Grassroots Out website pretty much summed up what the campaign to leave the EU was all about. Liam Fox explained that the EU was a threat to UK security, saying,

> Insecurity for our country comes from open borders and uncontrolled migration…Germany has discovered in Cologne and other places exactly what it may mean when you do not know who you have allowed into your country.[7]

One could not help wondering how Gorgeous George was going to sell that one to the UK Muslims! Fox went on to say that Britain had been 'able to save the European Continent twice from their own folly.'[8] That was an extremely simplistic, disingenuous and downright dishonest view of the two World Wars.

Tory MP Peter Bone, meanwhile, wrote of the 'Eurozone's worsening economic state and 'the migrant crisis' as reasons for wanting to leave the EU.[9] It looked as if the major gist of the Grassroots Out argument was that we were going to be swamped by immigrants, asylum seekers and refugees if we stayed in the EU. Ian Duncan Smith, Secretary of State for Works and Pensions, put a quasi-official, government stamp on this argument by saying that staying in the EU would make the UK vulnerable to Paris-style attacks.[10] It seemed a pretty poor basis for a campaign.

Unfortunately, the campaign to remain in the EU did not appear to be any better. David Cameron said that leaving would be a 'great leap in the dark' and claimed that British businesses would face uncertainty and possibly be faced with having to pay tariffs on exports.[11] Other arguments were that British workers could lose many of the rights they currently take for granted[12] while ex-pats living in Europe could lose pension rights.[13] As Anand Menon, professor of European politics at King's College London, said, 'This is going to be a depressingly negative campaign.'[14]

So, for the best part of five months the UK public was going to be exposed to a campaign with both sides telling them what they had to lose and very little about what there was to gain either by staying in Europe or leaving. By the time June 23rd came along, everyone would be heartily sick of the whole thing. In fact, they would be fed up long before that and the Holyrood elections could end up suffering accordingly.

It was clear from the Grassroots Out website what the main point of their campaign was going to be and at whom it was aimed. It is one of the banes of every Socialist's life that the 'oppressed masses' are often easily misdirected into blaming an ethnic, or religious, minority for their troubles, rather than their 'capitalist oppressors'. It is a lazy, evil strategy for politicians to use; unfortunately, it is also, more often than not, highly effective. It was obvious that Grassroots Out, and other Euro-sceptics, were going to try and motivate the dispossessed and disconnected by blaming immigrants for everything wrong and, in turn, by blaming the EU for foisting those immigrants upon us. A bit of religious, and racial, bigotry in the shape of Islamophobia was thrown in for good measure.

The big hope for David Cameron and those that wanted to stay in the EU was that a long and boring campaign would turn off the poorer sections of society. Such folk tend not to vote anyway and it takes a lot to motivate them; something that Grassroots Out and the rest hoped to do. It was doubtful that they would listen to reasoned arguments so boring them to death was the best chance of getting rid of a large chunk of anti-EU voters.

Unfortunately, as we have seen, these disaffected, and normally uninterested, voters were part of what helped make Scotland's Westminster representation almost wholly SNP. If the dispossessed in England were put off voting, then there was every chance that those in Scotland might be put off as well. The loss of SNP voters, however, would suit David Cameron and the Westminster Tories immensely.

The nightmare scenario for the Tories, and Labour too for that matter, was England voting to leave while Scotland elected to stay in the EU. An SNP government at Holyrood, with a large majority, would compound the issue and possibly lead to another Scottish referendum. Even well-known Euro-sceptics like William Hague could see the danger and had decided to support staying in the EU to prevent the break-up of the UK.[15] But why were the Tories so desperate to hold onto Scotland?

This was a question that had vexed many supporters of Scottish independence during the 2014 Referendum and nobody could give them a clear-cut answer. It was a reasonable enough question, given that English people were utterly convinced that the whole of Scotland practically lived off their taxes. With the oil nearly finished and the price at rock bottom, why did they not just let us go?

You might remember the story about David Cameron visiting Shetland during the Scottish Referendum campaign; the first prime minister in thirty-four years to do so. He, his office, Alistair Carmichael and the media were at pains to tell us that his visit had nothing to do with oil or gas discoveries.[16] Nobody bothered to tell us exactly what Cameron *was* doing there, so the conspiracy theories never went away.

There was still plenty of oil to be had in the North Sea[17] and, in February 2016 new gas fields off Shetland were announced.[18] It was estimated that these new finds could supply the whole of Scotland for the next twenty years. More pointedly, the BBC stated that the fields would 'produce about 8% of the UK's gas needs.'[19] Obviously Westminster still needed to siphon off the riches coming from Scotland's natural resources. The low oil prices could not stay that way forever, so there were still pressing reasons for Scotland to remain part of the UK. It was clear that the conspiracy theorists had been right about Cameron's Shetland jaunt.

The plan for having the EU Referendum campaign running at the same time as the campaigning for the Holyrood elections, therefore, made perfect sense. Confusion and overkill would combine to put off those least likely to vote; giving the double advantage of holding the Euro-sceptics at bay while possibly reducing the SNP's hegemony at Holyrood. This would avoid the nightmare envisioned by William Hague and others.

The Tories know full well that their chances of making gains in Scotland in general elections are practically non-existent. They are more than happy to let us return SNP members to Westminster from now until doomsday, as it helps keep Labour from getting into power. The Scottish Government, however, is a different matter entirely. Again, there is never going to be a Tory majority so the ideal situation would be a Labour government. Such a government would be much more malleable; having to keep one eye on not alienating potential Labour voters in England. In negotiations with Westminster, an SNP government, on the other hand, has nothing to lose and everything to gain.

We can see, then, what the strategies were of the right-wing elements in England, on both sides of the argument about the EU. But what about the left wing; more specifically, the left wing in Scotland that supports independence? What would be their take on whether or not to stay in the EU?

The Left has always had a rather ambivalent attitude towards Europe and many of those that did not want to join the Common Market in the 1970s were in the Labour Party. Ever since then, opinion has been divided between those that see the EU as in the control of the banks and those that welcome the workers' rights legislation that the EU has passed. This legislation is a major point in the EU's favour since it is extremely doubtful that Westminster would ever have passed such laws.

RISE, by March 2016, seemed reluctant to commit itself one way or the other. The Bella Caledonia website, however, showed what at least some in the organisation were thinking. Apparently, there was a new, pan-European movement taking shape, looking to democratise the EU and prise it out of the control of the bankers. The writer of this article waxed lyrical about the opportunity this new movement presented:

> The timing of this new, pan-European initiative could not be better for the Scottish Left as it faces the prospect of the EU referendum, and the mass mobilization (sic) date of May 28th, not even a month from the referendum, is an excellent potential rallying point for the Scottish Left to position itself regarding the European question. For the problem for the Scottish Left must surely be how to get enthusiastic about a campaign which it never wanted in the first place, and to be caught in the strange circumstance of being on the same side of the argument as people like PM Cameron or Junker, the Head of the European Commission.[20]

It looked, then, as if RISE would probably be in favour of staying in the EU. Tommy Sheridan's Solidarity party, however, was a different story. Their website made it plain that they would be campaigning to get us out of what the writer called 'Big Business EU'.[21] It was emphasised, in case there was any doubt, that Solidarity

> distance ourselves from the narrow-minded right-wing stance adopted by such organisations as UKIP and certain Conservative politicians, with whom we will not share a platform in this campaign.[22]

Strangely, Solidarity was standing in the Holyrood elections on a platform that included Scottish independence and another independence referendum in 2018.[23] If, as they were asking, a majority in Scotland voted to leave the EU, then an important argument for having another independence referendum would disappear. It was a strangely contradictory set of policies to put before the electorate.

Interestingly, though, Tommy Sheridan had indicated that this was going to be his last attempt to get elected. If he failed this time, then he was going to retire from politics.[24] Possibly he had decided to cross his own, particular Rubicon and, as Julius Caesar put it, stake it all on one throw of the dice. After all, he would probably have no chance at all if he was offering nothing different from RISE.

Perhaps this campaign to leave the EU was not as silly as it first appeared. Politicians are often accused of underestimating the intelligence and understanding of the electorate. The opposite, however, can also be true and some folk can pick up completely the wrong end of the stick. One Scottish independence supporter on a newspaper forum, for example, said, 'If you want an Independent Scotland - vote for Brexit.'[25] Quite how he, or she, arrived at that conclusion the commenter neglected to inform us.

This commenter was not alone in believing what he did; he was in some good company. Like some bitter ex-lover, Jim Sillars, one-time deputy leader of the SNP, appeared in the press to undermine the current party's position. He said,

> The UK remaining within the EU is self-evidently

counter-productive to the independence movement; the idea that Scotland voting to stay, while England and the rest vote to leave, would trigger a referendum is not only fanciful but undermined by the SNP decision to take the debate down south.[26]

Sillars was not the only one to condemn Nicola Sturgeon for launching her 'EU Remain' in London. The Daily Express was almost apoplectic with rage that a Scottish politician would have the gall to come to London 'to preach to English people about how they should vote in the Referendum.'[27] With a barefaced cheek that takes one's breath away, the paper continued:

> Ms Sturgeon ran what was dubbed "a remorselessly negative campaign" against the UK in the Scottish independence referendum where she tried to scare Scottish voters into leaving Britain by claiming that remaining would kill the NHS.
> But despite her tactics in 2014, Ms Sturgeon warned Prime Minister David Cameron that he should not follow her example and run Project Fear in trying to keep the UK in the EU.[28]

The comments at the end of the article were full of exhortations to Sturgeon to 'go back to Scotland', again raising questions of what the whole 'Better Together' campaign was all about. Scotland had voted in the Referendum the way that England had wanted and now they should get back in the box and shut up.

In fact, Sturgeon was only doing what all our media had been demanding that everyone connected with the YES campaign in the Referendum do; moving on. The majority of Scottish voters had chosen to remain in the UK and Nicola Sturgeon was in charge of a party that now almost completely represented the Scottish people at Westminster. Surely it was her duty, as leader of a Westminster party, to campaign throughout the UK for what she believed?

It was also another example of the SNP putting the

needs of the country before the needs of the party, which would be better served by England voting to leave the EU. The hypocrisy of the Unionist parties and media was evident. They had wanted Scotland to stay in the UK but were vilifying a Scottish politician for campaigning on an issue that affected the whole UK.

As for Jim Sillars, English Euro-sceptics were quick to point out that he had actually been one of the ones that had formulated the SNP policy of Scottish independence in Europe.[29] If he had changed his mind, then it proved that it was in Scotland's best interests to leave the EU. Sillars himself was emphatic about why Scottish nationalists should vote to leave. 'Staying in the EU keeps us in the trap of EU hostility to Scottish member state status, expressed so forcibly in 2014.'[30] As anyone that paid attention during the Scottish Independence Referendum knows, that was a blatant untruth; the EU had expressed no such hostility.

The stance of Jim Sillars and Tommy Sheridan, of course, was all grist to the Tories' mill; the more splits there were in the Scottish independence vote the better. Anyone that doubted why Cameron had called for the EU Referendum to take place when he had only needed to look at two things: the timing and the rush with which Cameron carried out his negotiations in Europe.

If anything was learned by the Unionist side in the Scottish Independence Referendum, it was that relying on a purely negative campaign is a rather dangerous road to go down. Westminster was offering nothing whatsoever during the campaign except scaremongering about what would happen if we left the UK. Eventually, sense was seen and a programme of reforms, the Vow, was produced, albeit illegally by the terms of the election rules. The Vow helped to swing many voters away from the YES side; for the EU Referendum, though, it might be better not to wait until the last minute.

Strangely, however, Cameron only spent two days in Brussels negotiating[31] and hardly made much of a fuss in the media about what he had supposedly achieved. In fact, Cameron had nothing but negative comments about leaving the EU to offer, as well as attacking those in his party that would be campaigning to exit Europe.[32] If he had been serious about wanting something positive to put before the voters, would he not have spent far more time negotiating in Brussels? After all, the next general election did not have to take place until 2020; he had four years in which to hold the referendum. Why the big hurry?

The only possible answer is that the referendum needed to be timed to run consecutively with the Holyrood elections. Cameron might want to stay in the EU but his main priority had to be to keep Scotland in the UK, for the reasons outlined above. He, and others in his party, hoped that the 'Brexit' campaign would have an influence on the elections for the Scottish Parliament, to the detriment of the SNP.

Quite apart from this political chicanery, the EU Referendum showed the complete hypocrisy of the Unionist politicians and media. On 16th February the Daily Mail published a story about actress Emma Thompson saying that we should not leave the EU. The paper said that 'She has never been afraid of spouting her London metropolitan elite views on matters of political importance.'[33] Meanwhile, Tory politicians took to Twitter to call her an 'overpaid Leftie luvvie' and the 'worst sort of fat-cat luvvie', accused her of venting 'metropolitan elitist snobbery' and said that 'If she hates our country so much she is very welcome to leave.'[34]

The contrast with the Scottish Independence Referendum was startling. The same crowd that wanted 'luvvies' to keep their noses out had been desperate to highlight the support of such 'luvvies' for Scotland remaining in the UK in 2014. And it was not just showbiz folk that were to keep out of the EU debate.

The Daily Express had a piece on November 5th 2015 expressing outrage at what it saw as the Obama administration getting involved in the EU Referendum. Nigel Farage condemned the 'political interference by the Obama regime in the British referendum', adding, 'I am outraged at his (U.S. Trade Representative Michael Froman's) level of interference'.[35] Then, in January 2016, Tory euro-sceptic Philip Hollobone demanded in the House of Commons 'that it would be made clear to the U.S. ambassador that the president should not be commenting on very important domestic issues, important to the people of this country.'[36]

What a difference from the Scottish Independence Referendum, where everyone from the Pope to the Chinese Premier was invited to put in their tuppence-worth. This time round we even had financial 'legend' Peter Hargreaves blasting the Governor of the Bank of England for getting involved on the side of those wanting to stay in the EU.[37] Of course, nobody in our media pointed out the irony of this point of view.

There was another matter that would vex those campaigning to leave Europe; the votes of the more than two million British ex-pats living and, in some cases, working across the EU. It was by no means certain that all the ex-pats would vote to remain in Europe; one character, living in Cyprus, maintained that a poll on his website for ex-pats showed that 65% of them wanted to leave the EU.[38] It was generally thought, however, that British ex-pats would vote to stay in Europe; their own self-interest would demand it.[39]

The fact was that many ex-pats would not be able to vote at all; only those that had lived abroad for fifteen years or less were eligible. Moves were afoot to abolish this rule but David Cameron seemed to be in no hurry to put this 'Votes for Life' bill before Parliament.[40] This placed a huge question mark over Cameron's commitment to staying in Europe, a point which was of concern to some American politicians.[41] At any rate, many ex-pats would be ineligible to vote in the referendum; something that would please those seeking to leave the EU.

A related issue was that of foreign nationals living in the UK. For years this had been a bugbear of British right-wingers, who argued that it was undemocratic.[42] The EU Referendum was of particular concern in this respect as it was fairly obvious which way migrant workers from Europe would vote. The bill setting up the EU Referendum calmed these fears by excluding most Europeans living in Britain from voting in it.[43] This, however, was not enough for many right-wingers.

Migration Watch UK, an independent, right-wing think-tank, was concerned that there were still over one-and-a-half million foreigners eligible to vote in the referendum. These were people from Ireland and the Commonwealth.[44] No doubt there would be complaints galore from certain quarters if these voters helped to keep Britain in the EU. Again, however, this would be extremely hypocritical.

A study of how people voted in the Scottish Independence Referendum showed that folk born in other parts of the UK were much more likely to vote NO than those born in Scotland.[45] Nobody in the SNP complained about this; as far as they were concerned everyone living in Scotland was entitled to a say. In the opinion of a lot of English right-wingers, it appeared, however, that it should be one rule for a referendum on Scottish independence, but quite another when it came to voting on leaving the EU.

While these arguments among right-wingers were taking place, just like RISE, Scottish Labour, and, indeed, the Labour Party UK-wide, was remarkably muted in its support for staying in the EU. This was hardly surprising since the leadership was allowing the party's members to choose whichever side they wished to support.[46] In fact, there was already a 'Labour Leave' organisation set up, which hoped to get Labour MSPs onside.[47] The Labour-supporting press in Scotland was quiet about Europe as well. It had bigger fish to fry; like attacking the SNP for its 'austerity' budget.

10
Austerity Verities

On February 25th, the day after John Swinney gave his budget statement at Holyrood, the Daily Record had this headline on its editorial page: 'John Swinney had the chance to prove he wasn't Osborne Mark 2...he failed'.[1] This was a recurring theme in the Scottish media and in statements by Scottish Labour and RISE. The accusation was that the Scottish Government was doing the Tories' dirty work and making sure that Scotland did not escape Westminster's austerity measures.

When agreement had been reached to allow the Scotland Bill to be put to the House of Commons, the announcement was greeted, you may remember, by Kezia Dugdale in the following way:

> Now that an agreement has been reached every single political party in Scotland must focus on what we can do with these major new powers. The opportunities they provide are huge – we can use the new tax and welfare powers to bring an end to Tory austerity and build a fairer country.[2]

The Daily Record, while patting itself on the back over the Vow and insinuating that the new powers were being delivered *in spite* of the SNP, had this to say:

> Now the debate must move on from technical arguments, away from process, and on to what Scotland

and Scotland's government will do with the powers. The time for "if" has passed. Now we need the "when".

And with the SNP certain to be returned to power in May's Scottish elections, it will fall to Sturgeon to spell out how she will use Holyrood's new powers to benefit ordinary Scots.[3]

Scottish Labour and the Daily Record, however were being completely disingenuous about these new powers; in fact, one could go further and accuse them of being bare-faced liars. They were as aware as the SNP that the much-vaunted new powers would not come into force until 2017 at the earliest.[4] Calls for the Scottish Government to use its new powers immediately were nothing more than publicity-seeking soundbites; they knew full well that the Scottish Government was unable to comply.

The new powers would allow the Scottish Government to set its own tax bands but, as things stood in February 2016, any tax increase would have to be levied across the board. A 1p increase may not sound much but to a family living on a wage of £15,000 a year it would mean having about £12 a month less; something which it could ill afford.

Scottish Labour's madcap scheme to administer £100 rebates would never work. It would be akin to setting new tax bands by the back door and would be easily challenged by the Tory Party in court. Scottish Labour was promising something that it knew it would never have to deliver, while dishonestly attempting to make the SNP look bad.

While Labour MSPs in Scotland were accusing the SNP of being the Tories' partner in austerity, their colleagues in Westminster were hardly acting as a vanguard in opposing the UK Government. In fact, the party leadership was doing precisely nothing. During the summer of 2015, interim leader, Harriet Harman, ordered Labour MPs to abstain from voting on the Government's Welfare Bill, the Tory Budget and the SNP amendment to deny the Budget a second reading.[5]

To their credit, 48 Labour MPs defied the party whip and voted against the Welfare Bill, expressing shame at how the leadership was acting.[6] The party even used the whip to get Labour MPs to abstain when the Government introduced measures to scrap the 'purdah' period in the EU Referendum. Several Tory MPs voted against the Government, along with the SNP, which meant that if Labour had participated the measure would have been defeated. This prompted Alex Salmond to say, 'Labour have yet again chosen to abstain on a key vote – they need to find a backbone and become an effective opposition in parliament.'[7]

The only excuse the Labour Party had was that they did not have a leader yet, causing all manner of uncertainty. In September they got a leader, though not the one the parliamentary party would have liked. Jeremy Corbyn, a left-winger, won the first round by a landslide.[8] The Parliamentary Labour Party probably did not know whether to laugh or cry. Corbyn's election led to thousands flocking to join the party[9], which was a cheering sight but Corbyn had made it plain that it was the party membership that would be determining policy;[10] that was hardly going to endear the new leader to the PLP.

New members of the party were all very well but to the PLP it was votes that counted; votes which they could not help but think that Corbyn was going to lose them. In fact, there had been stories that many of the new members that had selected Corbyn were actually Tories, voting for what they hoped would be an unelectable Labour leader.[11] The surge in membership after Corbyn's victory, however, somewhat belies this viewpoint. When the dust had settled Labour now had a left-wing leader, backed by a left-wing membership, but a parliamentary party still full of Blairites. It looked as if there would be nothing but trouble ahead.

Trouble was avoided, however, due to the fact that Corbyn turned out to be a rather weak leader. It seemed he was either unwilling or unable to use the whip, even when he had the overwhelming support of the party membership. Apparently 75% of Labour members polled were against air strikes on Syria; Corbyn, however, backed down to pressure from the PLP and allowed a free vote.[12] It looked as if the same thing was going to happen in the upcoming debate about renewing Trident.[13]

So, while Labour at Holyrood was accusing the SNP of inflicting austerity on Scotland, their colleagues at Westminster were doing nothing whatsoever to oppose austerity affecting the whole UK. In fact, many of them were in favour of wasting tax-payers' money on nuclear weapons and pointless air raids on Syria.

We have seen already how Scottish Labour's agenda of blaming the SNP for austerity was based on the funding from the Scottish Government to local councils. They criticised the amount given to councils and health boards without taking account of from where, in a limited budget, the Scottish Government was supposed to find extra cash. Also, they completely ignored how their own party was failing to oppose austerity measures at Westminster; measures that impacted on the block grant that Holyrood received.

The constraints on local government spending was not just due to the lack of funds coming from Holyrood or the freeze on council tax; other factors played a part. The law said that all councils had to balance their budgets;[14] something large councils with many poverty-stricken residents found it extremely difficult to do. Thirteen years of Labour government at Westminster had not really helped them very much.

In fact, Labour had actually compounded the problems of councils and health boards with its PFI schemes. The Labour Party, both at Holyrood and Westminster, had involved the private sector in the building of new hospitals and schools. Everybody was grateful, of course, for the brand-spanking new buildings and facilities, but they came at a high cost. Councils and health boards were landed with debts that were going to take decades to clear, as well as binding contracts for cleaning and other ancillary services.[15]

There is another problem that nobody likes to talk about; one which has been around ever since the old regional councils were disbanded in 1996. This problem is most evident in parts of what was once Strathclyde Region. East Dunbartonshire Council is quite affluent compared to other councils and contains Bearsden and Milngavie, where some of the most expensive property in Scotland can be found. Despite the wealth concentrated in these two districts, homeowners pay less council tax than their near-neighbours in Glasgow.

Council-tax bands are uniform throughout Scotland and

Band H applies to all homes that were worth over £212,000 in 1991.[16] Houses built since then are assessed based on what they would have been worth in 1991. Glasgow currently has 662 Band H properties and 6,070 Band G properties, which are worth between £106,000 and £212,000 at 1991 prices. This is out of a total of 300,000 residential properties.[17]

In Bearsden and Milngavie, it is quite a different matter. Out of a total of 16,896 properties in 2013, there were 4,536 at Band G and 517 at Band H.[18] It is reasonable to assume that there has not been a lot of change since then; certainly none of these properties would have decreased in value. And these are just two areas in East Dunbartonshire. Altogether, in the same year, East Dunbartonshire Council had 44,775 properties, of which 6075 were at Band G and 591 at Band H.[19] It is obviously a far more well-off area than Glasgow, with relatively low unemployment.[20]

Turning back to Bearsden and Milngavie, you would be hard-pushed to find any social housing in these areas. In 2013 there were only 143 properties at Band A and 147 at Band B.[21] With all the social housing and areas of deprivation in Glasgow it would be no surprise to find that there are many thousands of Band A and Band B properties in the city. With next to no unemployment in Bearsden and Milngavie, the council can be sure of collecting all that it is owed, with hardly any rebates due. In fact, this is the case throughout East Dunbartonshire.

With less of a population, East Dunbartonshire Council does not need to provide as many facilities as Glasgow, which means they can charge less council tax. Since the new local authorities were set up in 1996, council tax has been consistently lower in East Dunbartonshire than in Glasgow. In 2015/16 those five-hundred-odd Level H properties in Bearsden and Milngavie paid nearly £150 a year less than their counterparts in Glasgow.[22] [23]

This appears, on the surface, to be fair enough; folk in Bearsden and Milngavie have less facilities than those in Glasgow so it stands to reason that they should pay less. The problem is, however, that the reason why these two areas do not have facilities is because they do not need them; they use those in Glasgow. Concert recitals at Kelvingrove Art Gallery are full of people from Bearsden in Milngavie, who book their seats well in advance. Events at parks and libraries, Zumba classes at sports centres, squash courts, golf courses; you will find people from Bearsden and Milngavie at them all. They worm their way in due to the fact that most of them work in Glasgow. Residents of the posh areas in the west of the city are never done moaning about it.

The Tories were never going to do anything about this anomaly and the Labour Party left it well alone when it was in power at Westminster. The Scottish Government can do nothing about this unfairness; only independence would bring it such powers.

In the meantime, the calls continued for the council-tax freeze to be lifted so that councils could raise more money for schools etc. It was either that or Scottish Labour's insane and unworkable income-tax scheme. Nicola Sturgeon and her party held firm; if they put any tax up at the present time, then everyone, rich and poor, would be hit. Finally, though, there was some light at the end of the tunnel for local authorities.

Nicola Sturgeon's announcement, at the beginning of March 2016, that the freeze on council tax would end the following year, rather pulled the rug from under the feet of the SNP's opponents.[24] Councils were going to be able to increase the tax by up to 3% a year, while the charges on properties between Band E and Band H were going to be raised.[25] It was as the Scottish Government had kept telling everyone; all the new tax powers in the Scotland Bill would not be available until 2017.

Of course, not everyone was happy. COSLA called the plans a 'damp squib' and a 'missed opportunity'.[26] Jackie Baillie, as usual, had plenty to say on the subject:

> The SNP promised to abolish council tax back in 2007 and attacked Labour's proposals to change the way banding worked. Yet that is exactly what the SNP Government has announced today. It has taken the SNP a decade to deliver tinkering round the edges rather than real reform.
>
> In the longer term the SNP's plan to assign rates of income tax to local authorities seems unfair given the

huge difference between the amount of income tax paid between areas, and it will do little to encourage economic development in cities where large sections of the workforce come from neighbouring local authorities.[27]

Also as usual, Baillie had no alternative to offer; neither did anybody else. In fact, the cross-party Commission on Local Tax Reform had recommended in 2015 that the council tax be replaced by something fairer. Again, though, the Commission failed to come up with any idea of what it should be replaced with.[28] Rather than blame this useless commission, which had spent ages, and tax-payers' money, just to reach a conclusion that would have taken any person in the street five minutes to come up with, everyone pointed the finger at the SNP.

Everything that Jackie Baillie was moaning about was outwith the control of the Scottish Government. As we have seen, local authority borders would have to be redrawn; something that only Westminster could do. Baillie was as aware of that as anyone. She was also aware that her own party had done absolutely nothing about these anomalies when it was in power.

Our elected government found itself in the firing line yet again. The Labour Party was happy to let the Tories make all their cuts virtually unopposed, while its members in Scotland tried to blame the SNP. Scottish Labour, and its friends in the media, were also blaming the Scottish Government for matters over which it had no control. And even when the Government at Holyrood responded to calls and set out plans to raise more money, everyone did nothing but complain. Not one critic came up with a viable alternative; but, then, nobody asked them to. Blaming the SNP had become so ingrained that it was all that was required to be considered an effective opposition.

Speaking of opposition, RISE was still looking to replace Labour in this position at Holyrood. Unfortunately, taking on Labour's mantle also seemed to involve inheriting some of the cynicism that had led to the party's demise in Scotland. It was time for RISE to try to win votes using any means possible.

11
Playing The Green Card

Cynicism necessarily plays a large part in politics. If you want to get into power, there are party colleagues to bring onside and voters to manipulate. No matter how sincere you are about the good you want to do, you have to play the game by the same rules as everybody else. It seems as if it has always been that way. Gladstone was determined to implement independence for Ireland and needed the support of his whole party to do so. He promised the earth to different sections of the Liberal Party, as long as they were prepared to support Irish independence as the priority. Harold Wilson pretty much used the same tactics to hold the disparate elements of the Labour Party together. He was such an expert that he could even convince the Americans that he was right behind them on Vietnam while keeping Britain well out of it.

The SNP is not above such cynicism and constantly has to strive to get our antagonistic media to treat it fairly. John Swinney probably had to grit his teeth and hold his nose when he thanked the Daily Record for its 'help' during the 'financial framework' negotiations.[1] This was totally at odds with how the Record had really behaved during this spell. Politically, however, Swinney could do nothing else.

Sometimes politicians will appeal to racism and bigotry to get votes. During the Scottish Independence Referendum campaign, the phrase 'break-up of the United Kingdom' was almost a code, appealing to Orange sentiment in our country. The big fear was that Scottish independence would lead to increased calls in Northern Ireland to leave the UK.[2] It was only stated explicitly in a few places but the message was always there in the background. The march by Ulster Orangemen in Edinburgh and the disgusting scenes in Glasgow on the day after the vote showed how much this message had penetrated.

The EU Referendum appeared to be going down the same route. It is interesting to note that the Euro-sceptic scare stories about border controls said nothing about Eastern Europeans coming here to work. Instead, the emphasis was on refugees and asylum seekers.[3] Read the comments in the Daily Mail, the Express or the Telegraph and you will see nonsense galore about swarms of Muslims coming into the UK and about us all ending up under Sharia Law. It was to this type of bigot that Grassroots Out in particular was appealing.

One thing about most bigots is that they will argue until they are blue in the face that bigotry plays no part whatsoever in their beliefs or actions. Often the bigotry is couched in terms where the bigots themselves attempt to play the victims. One such ruse is the ridiculous argument that, soon, the whole country is going to be taken over by foreigners; more specifically, black-faced foreigners. The views expressed by such folk are hilarious but, at the same time, quite frightening. An example is this comment, written without a hint of irony:

And Europe and America belong to White Europeans. Blacks would be happier in their own miserable 3rd world nations which wiull (sic) be further decayed in a decade, typical negro behavior (sic) of course. So why dont (sic) they all leave and expatriate to coastal Africa?[4]

Sometimes an official or an academic will appear to lend some authoritative credence to this rubbish. Step forward Professor David Coleman of Oxford University, who was banging on about this stuff even back in 2010.[5] Professor Coleman is also a co-founder of anti-immigration pressure group, Migration Watch and a member of the Galton Institute, the new name for the British Eugenics Society.[6]

That probably tells you all you need to know about Professor David Coleman.

Now and again this racism comes out into the open, embarrassing everyone in authority and in the media, who all rush to condemn it. On the whole, however, the Establishment is happy enough to condone it, as long as its exponents keep up a respectable front.

Scotland likes to pretend that racism does not exist here and that it is not as big a problem as it is in England. The latter is certainly true, although the main reason for that is the fact that there are a lot less black people in Scotland, even looking at the figures proportionally. Besides, Scotland has had, for a long time now, somebody else to take the brunt of the racism, bigotry and paranoia: Irish Catholics.

The Church of Scotland published a pamphlet in 1923, called, 'The Menace of the Irish race to our Scottish Nationality'. It was made plain that it was specifically Irish Catholics that were the problem; Irish Protestants were a different matter. As the pamphlet put it:

> [no complaint can be made about] the presence of an Orange population in Scotland. They are of the same race as ourselves and of the same Faith, and are readily assimilated to the Scottish race.[7]

The general consensus is that this sectarian and racist bigotry has all but disappeared; many, however, are not convinced. It is easy to find individuals and organisations on the internet that believe that anti-Irish and anti-Catholic bigotry are an institutional problem in Scotland, just as others maintain that racism based on colour is institutionalised in England. When one sees and hears thousands singing bigoted songs at football matches with impunity, it is often hard to argue with this assessment.

Possibly a more telling sign of how ingrained anti-Irish sentiment is in Scotland was shown by a sports journalist in the Daily Record as recently as 2008. Reporting on the furore surrounding the singing of 'The Famine Song' by Rangers supporters, this journalist suggested that anyone offended by it should 'Go.'[8] Imagine what would have happened if he had made that suggestion to folk of Pakistani descent!

In England and America accusations of institutional racism are usually countered by pointing to black people in positions of power. The same thing happens in Scotland, where there are politicians, councillors, businessmen etc. of Irish-Catholic descent. In all these cases, however, the claims are rather disingenuous. In the USA in 2013 12% of the population was black and yet black people made up 40% of those in prison.[9] It looked from figures released in 2014 that England was headed in the same direction.[10] The fact is that, both in the UK and the USA, black people tend to be poorer than white people and it is these folk that have to bear the brunt of any racism, institutionalised or not.

In Scotland it is not black people that are over-represented in prisons; it is Roman Catholics. Some commentators blamed this on sectarianism in the justice system[11], while others saw it as more a matter of Catholics being disproportionally resident in areas of poverty and deprivation.[12] Either way, it was a shameful indictment of Scottish society.

Historian, and Roman Catholic, Tom Devine might argue that viewing this as discrimination was just promoting a 'lingering sense of victimhood',[13] but it has to be said that he, in his academic ivory tower and with his middle-class lifestyle, will not have to suffer the bigotry and hatred that working-class Catholics have to face.

I, myself, experienced such discrimination when I was young, most especially when working in a bakers' factory while on holiday from university one summer. A delivery man, when he discovered my name, made jokes about me being Catholic and Irish; the jokes stopped, however, when he dropped a sack of flour, which burst open. My gaffers had to hide me in the store, behind sacks of flour etc., until the man had eaten his lunch and gone. He blamed 'That papish bastard, Paddy' for the loss of the sack of flour and threatened to give me the beating of a lifetime. As a skinny, wee seventeen-year-old I was no match for the hulking, great brute.

Like Tom Devine, I was able to go to university and escape

into a middle-class profession. Others, however, were not quite so lucky and would have had to put up with characters like that delivery man their whole lives. It would be easy for me, like Devine, to scoff at claims of discrimination. I, however, do not believe that the problem has gone away just because I happen to be no longer personally affected.

We have already looked at how many socialists from middle-class backgrounds try to disguise the fact, somehow believing that it might diminish their credibility. They will go to any lengths to pretend that they come from a working-class background. Such a one is Cat Boyd, trade-unionist, socialist and RISE list candidate for the 2016 Holyrood elections. (Apropos what was discussed in Chapter 7, have a guess at Boyd's favourite book.[14])

Details of Boyd's background are, understandably, scarce, but her mother is a high-flying educationalist with North Lanarkshire Council, who was awarded a CBE for her work.[15] Coming from a middle-class background does not disbar one from being a socialist; to suggest that it does is ridiculous snobbery. Hiding one's background, however, is quite duplicitous. Boyd makes great play of working 'in a low paid area'[16] and starting 'for the Department for Work and Pensions in 2008 as a low-ranking civil servant'.[17] She neglects to mention, however, that, with a degree from Strathclyde University, she probably had better options available.[18]

Like my own daughter, Boyd probably never had to experience the anti-Catholic and anti-Irish bigotry that others have had to put up with. She, however, begged to differ and wrote an article in the National to prove her point.[19]

She is certainly right about the scandal of there being no St Patrick's Day celebrations in Glasgow, while the rest of the world has a party. As we saw earlier with the situation in North Lanarkshire, the very idea of anything Irish sends some folk into paroxysms of fury. To these folk, holding any kind of official party or parade would be nothing short of treachery.

Unfortunately, while acknowledging the racial bigotry still endemic against Irish people in Scotland, Boyd makes the mistake of coming out with this categorical statement:

the days where having an Irish name constituted a real barrier to getting a job in the private sector are more or less gone. There's racism in Scotland, but the Irish very rarely take the brunt of it.[20]

The question has to be asked: how does she know? Just because there are no notices anymore, saying, 'RCs need not apply' or 'No dogs, no blacks, no Irish' does not mean that anti-Irish racism has disappeared. In the USA in the 1960s, the tactics used by the likes of the NAACP in the Southern states were useless in the Northern ones. Racism there was much more subtle; there were no special seats on the bus or in diners, but the racism was still there. Equally, just because anti-Irish racism is no longer as blatant does not mean that it has gone.

Would any other football manager go through what Neil Lennon did, only for the media to say that 'he brings it on himself'? And what of the facts that Catholic people of Irish descent are more likely to live in poverty and end up in prison? It is all very well to highlight folk that have done well but the same situation exists in America, where the fact that there is a 'niggra' in the White House somehow makes people believe that racism is a thing of the past.

Boyd attempts to answer this line of questioning by relating the tale of her encountering a gang of bigots on the Glasgow Underground, singing the 'Famine Song'. She confronted them and was called a 'Fenian bitch' for her trouble; meanwhile, the other passengers looked away. She puts down the bigots' reply down to this: 'By some sixth sense, they must have been able to detect my generations-old ethnic heritage'.[21] Perhaps she is being ironic, but the fact is that even if she had been black, with a Botswana accent and wearing a large Star of David round her neck, she would still have been called a 'Fenian bitch'.

So why had Ms Boyd decided to regale us with her Irish ancestry and being a victim of racial bigotry at this time? The answer was obvious; there was an election coming up. We have already seen the report that showed that Catholics were more likely to vote for independence than their Protestant neighbours,[22] so it could not hurt to try to get them onside. Boyd betrayed her intentions slightly when she said, 'I've got a modest proposal for Glasgow's *middle-class* civic leaders. Let's celebrate our city's Irish heritage, and be proud of it together – not be cowed by bigots.'[23] (Italics mine) Notice that; *middle-class* civic leaders – as opposed to 'us' working-class Catholics of Irish descent!

There is another point that Boyd did not mention; one that impacts directly on the Scottish Government. Boyd did not have to bring up this matter in her article; everybody that follows football in Scotland already knew about it.

The Offensive Behaviour at Football and Threatening Communications (Scotland) Act had been plagued by controversy ever since it was first passed. The ideas behind the Act were laudable[24] but everyone seemed to believe that it had been an abject failure. Football supporters held demonstrations and displayed banners at matches demanding the Act's abolishment; not least at Celtic Park.

Not all Celtic supporters are Catholic, but it is quite reasonable to state that most people of Irish-Catholic descent in Glasgow, at the very least, have a soft spot in their hearts for the club. It was, after all, founded to help the Irish-Catholic community and it still has strong links with the descendants of that community; the very ones to whom Cat Boyd was trying to appeal.

Boyd was not the only politician trying to gain capital in this area. Labour MSP James Kelly said, 'The Football Act is eroding trust between football fans and the police and that is solely because of the SNP.'[25] But was this, in fact, true? Was the failure of the act solely the responsibility of the SNP?

The Act was brought in specifically because the police, the judiciary, the SFA and football clubs themselves were doing nothing at all to stamp out some of the vile sectarian and racist bigotry evident at matches. Songs and chants that would get you charged, and probably convicted, of breach of the peace in normal circumstances seemed to be tolerated at football as just 'part of the atmosphere'. Since the Act was brought in, it seemed that none of these attitudes had changed.

What chance did the Act have when judges described it as

'mince'[26] and the police just stand and watch while thousands sing about being up to their knees in 'Fenian blood'?[27] Meanwhile, the media actually print guff about not singing the Billy Boys because it arms the 'social media vampires who feed off of hatred of the club and its culture.'[28] The football authorities and the club itself, as they had always done, refused to take any action at all over the incident.

One wonders if the reluctance to implement the Act stemmed from not wanting to expose Scotland's guilty secret or from the fact that it was an SNP government that introduced it. Probably it was a bit of both. It was obvious, whatever the reason, that Scotland's Establishment was determined that the legislation was going to fail. And, of course, the failure of the Act would be laid at the door of the Scottish Government.

Comments from Celtic supporters on newspaper and blog forums showed that there were many among them that viewed the implementation of the Act as discriminatory against them. (It has to be said that fans at Ibrox equally felt that it discriminated against *them*.) Rather than calling for more fairness, however, most Celtic supporters wanted the Act itself repealed. It was this sentiment that Cat Boyd was trying to manoeuvre into voting for her. After all, what could be more discriminatory than the Government passing laws against you?

And so, on the one hand we had the Scottish Establishment undermining the Scottish Government by ensuring that a law to stamp out bigotry was not going to work. On the other, we had politicians like Cat Boyd cynically using the situation for their own ends. The actions (or inactions) of the Establishment appeared to be working; it was going to be interesting to see if Cat Boyd's plan would work as well.

12
A Parcel Of Rogues

We have seen all the chicanery being employed, either consciously or unconsciously, to undermine the SNP Scottish Government and, by extension, make Scottish independence much less likely. It is time to take a look at some of the individuals involved in this process.

Like 1970s DJs, some media political commentators see themselves as celebrities, as famous and important as politicians themselves. Such a one was Tom Brown of the Daily Record, whom the paper described as 'legendary' when he came back from the grave to put his tuppence-worth in during the Independence Referendum campaign.[1] His 'legend', however, does not seem to have spread much beyond his own mind and the pages of the Daily Record.

Brown's place at the Daily Record has been taken by one Torcuil Crichton, who seems to view himself in much the same way as Brown did. He is billed as the 'Daily Record's man in Westminister (sic) who stalks the corridors of power in London looking for a Scottish angle on the big political issues.'[2] Reading his articles his love for himself comes across almost as much as his hatred for the SNP.

'Torcuil' is normally a pretty upper-class name in Scotland, borne by the sons of lords, who forever wear tartan and fill their endless leisure time by attending ceilidhs in draughty, old castles. The constant wearing of kilts and tartan frippery is essential to prove their Scottishness, since their speech and manner are indiscernible from those of their counterparts in England.

Crichton, it appears, is not from this kind of background. His Facebook page has pictures of forebears working on crofts[3], which may be a Cat Boyd-esque cover-up but we shall give him the benefit of the doubt. He comes from Lewis and is a Gaelic speaker, which is possibly what got him into the media in the first place.

He worked for the West Highland Free Press for five-and-a-half years, which perhaps explains his blind devotion to Labour and his rabid hatred of the SNP. After a short stint at the Herald, he joined the BBC as a director and producer.[4] That was quite a leap from being a journalist. That was where the Gaelic came in handy.

Gaelic television is a strange beast. Back in the 1980s you used to have to suffer the news in Gaelic while waiting for the next programme to come on. A stilted, uncomfortable-looking newsreader would introduce reports on fish, sheep and Caledonian-MacBrayne, while the reporters themselves would interview folk that seemed ill-at-ease about the subject they were discussing. You wondered sometimes if the interviewee was a security guard or something, possibly the only one in the building that spoke Gaelic. And that was what made it all seem so amateur; talent was not as big a priority as the ability to speak Gaelic. There simply were not enough Cathy MacDonalds to go round.

Despite the lack of talent on display, Gaelic television was laudably ambitious, with children's programmes and European current affairs being tackled. Cathy MacDonald, of course, appeared in practically everything, even the children's programmes, along with funny, wee men with beards and dungarees. The fun and games, however, were easily spoiled by a co-presenter with all the thespian ability of a Hygena wardrobe. Ewan Bain, for example, was a genius when it came to his cartoons, especially Angus Og. As an actor on children's programmes, however, he could quite easily have been replaced by an aspidistra. Still, as long as he could speak Gaelic, he was in. This was the environment that Torcuil Crichton turned up to as a twenty-nine-year-old in 1993.

The BBC has always had a 'jobs for the boys' philosophy. In the post-war years it was all about who you knew as old school, university and army chums were invited along to see if there was anything they could do. Lack of talent was no obstacle; all you needed was a plummy voice and the right connections. Such a philosophy still plays a large part at the BBC, where employment often depends on completing an internship; something that ordinary people cannot afford to do. The Gaelic department is probably not as incestuous as this, but the fact has always been that, necessarily, speaking Gaelic is the primary requisite; the job can be picked up as you go along.

Crichton is still involved in promoting Gaelic, being on the Board of Directors of the Gaelic Arts Agency, along with, who else, Cathy MacDonald.[5] The remit of this agency is spelled out on their website: 'Pròiseact Nan Ealan plays an important role within the Gaelic arts sector, contributing to initiatives that have helped to create vibrant and sustainable Gaelic arts provision.'[6] That sounds like the sort of thing that Bella Caledonia would champion.

There is something obscene about spending public money on the arts when there are people literally starving; not that you will hear Torcuil Crichton complaining. In the Daily Record, he joins the chorus of voices demanding tax rises on the rich to offset Westminster cuts, neglecting, of course, to mention that the Scottish Government cannot actually do such a thing until 2017 at the earliest. It seems he supports the Labour position of raising tax across the board,[7] no matter how this might affect ordinary people. Maybe he has a recitation of the poems of Ossian, the Gaelic Homer, he wants funding for.

Being the Record's man in 'Westminister', Crichton spends a lot of his time in London and appears to have fallen in love with the place, and become blinded to its many faults. He says, 'With over eight million people, generating about a fifth of the UK's GDP, London is the dynamo of the UK economy.'[8] It is easy to be dazzled by all the bright lights and big buildings but, in reality, London's prosperity is all smoke and mirrors. They make money in London, using other people's money to do it; playing the markets, financing foreign projects and snapping up shares in government services that have been, and are being, privatised. London's economy has more in common with the South Sea Bubble than the Industrial Revolution.

Being the wide-eyed, peasant ingénue in the Big Smoke might be a dream come true for Crichton but it does not make for great political analysis. The vast majority of his articles are just about how evil the SNP is with not a lot about Westminster. That is surely something he could easily do at home, instead of the Record paying for a flat in London!

Someone that does work from home is Alistair Cameron, Director of Scotland in Union. Cameron's group was just one of a few Unionist groups advocating tactical voting in the 2015 General Election,[9] although Natalie McGarry has inadvertently now given SIU more publicity than it could ever have hoped for.[10] (McGarry really needs to stay away from social media; the Scottish press is desperate to pounce on her for the least thing.)

Cameron works as a consultant in the financial services industry in Edinburgh and has served in the military.[11] Like others, precise information appears to be scarce; it is difficult to determine, for example, if the man is Scottish or not. He certainly sounds English and looks every inch the Tory ex-army officer.[12] He is reported, though, as having been a Liberal-Democrat; not that there is too much difference between Lib-Dems and Tories nowadays.

Cameron's SIU describes itself as 'a non-party movement which unites people around a positive view of Scotland in the UK, and assists them in taking action.'[13] The action the SIU assisted people in taking was anything but positive. It consisted of giving advice on the best candidate to vote for in each constituency to keep the SNP from being elected.[14] That, unfortunately, is about as positive as it gets with SIU; their tactic certainly failed to make much of an impact in the General Election.

With more people knowing about the group now, SIU would probably be hoping to have more of an effect on the Holyrood elections in 2016. They produced what they called a 'Charter of Holyrood' to set out what they were looking to achieve.[15] It is worth having a look at a couple of the five points of this Charter.

1. Move on from the referendum together.

As SIU puts it, 'Both sides agreed the 2014 referendum on independence would deliver a fair test and a decisive expression of the views of the people of Scotland.' Unfortunately, not everyone is convinced that it was a 'fair test' and it was made plain throughout 2014 that if Scotland voted for independence, the Unionists had no intention of 'moving on'. Politicians vowed to fight 'tooth and nail' to thwart Scottish independence; now, because the vote went their way, everyone was supposed to 'move on'.

2. Work together with the rest of the UK.

'Before the referendum, Alex Salmond and David Cameron signed the 'Edinburgh Agreement'. They most assuredly did, and part of that agreement was to abide by the usual rules of elections and respect a period of 'purdah', which is defined as 'the period of time immediately before elections or referendums when specific restrictions on the activity of civil servants are in place. The term 'pre-election period' is also used.'[16] The UK Government broke this agreement with its last-minute 'Vow' and SIU has a damned cheek to attempt to castigate the SNP by citing it.

There is other stuff about 'decency' in politics, resurrecting the myth that only those on the YES side in the Referendum employed intimidatory tactics. SIU also expresses concern about the growing 'politicising of civic Scotland'. Incredibly, they do not see the irony in these not-so-subtle digs when their Unionist, anti-SNP agenda is helping to divide Scotland as much as, if not more than, any nationalist.

Alistair Cameron, at a meeting in Glasgow in December 2015, outlined the main concerns of SIU:

We will remind people that political debates should be about tax, spending, health, welfare, security and the other functions of the state, rather than indulging empty separatist gestures at the expense of running the country properly.[17]

That was a huge change from a few months before, when Cameron was encouraging folk to ignore policies and just vote for whoever would keep the SNP out. Obviously the man's hypocrisy knows no bounds. The only positive things he had to say about being in the UK were all about 'the benefits of a British passport' and 'the influence we can have in the world as part of the UK.'[18] He had nothing at all to say about 'tax, spending, health and welfare'; the policies SIU was supposed to be concerned with.

He finished by rousing the faithful to 'all do our bit to demonstrate that the SNP do not speak for the majority of people in Scotland'.[19] In fact, the SNP speaks for the majority in Scotland far more than the Westminster Government speaks for the majority in the UK. But, then, that is outside SIU's agenda. He promised that SIU would not be running a tactical voting campaign this time round but, no doubt, they would still be 'advising' people about the best candidate to vote for to keep out the SNP. One wonders how many RISE candidates would be on that particular list as SIU look to split the independence vote.

Which leads us to our next personality, RISE member and editor of Bella Caledonia, Mike Small. Small is an author and activist, well-known in Anarchist and Generalist circles, especially since he worked with Murray Bookchin, an influential figure among Anarchists and Ecologists.[20] He was not much known outside of these circles but came more into the public limelight with his website, Bella Caledonia.

At first, this website was primarily focused on Scottish independence but has widened into touching on many different subjects, in keeping with Small's Generalist principles. We have already seen how the website promotes 'Scots' language and there is a literary and intellectual atmosphere about the site, though no topic seems to be out of bounds.

Reading the site is reminiscent of being among a group of intellectual Socialists, Communists or Anarchists at college, university or a trades-union congress. It used to amaze me at university why such characters did not study something practical, like computer programming, which would let them actually attack the hated Establishment. Instead, they tended to study philosophy and politics; it seemed that talking was all they wanted to do.

And, by God, the folk on Bella Caledonia can talk! The contributors write copious articles, most of which actually undermine the Scottish independence they profess to support. We have already looked at the site's promotion of 'real' Scots and the same thing is done with Gaelic. '*Ghetto na Gàidhlig*', the web page is called; propagating the same myth they maintain about Scots. Gaelic has not been 'ghettoised' at all; it nearly died out because folk stopped speaking it. If somebody in the Highlands and Islands has the choice between their child learning French at school, opening up employment opportunities abroad, or their child learning Gaelic, which would enable them to understand the football commentary on BBC Alba, which one do you think he would choose? That is why the language is disappearing; it has nothing to do with it being forced into oblivion.

This rather inward-looking philosophy of Scottish independence is easily seized on by the opponents of independence. The SNP portrays itself as a modern, forward-looking party, something that the ideas expressed on Bella Caledonia undermine. One of the bugbears expressed on the website is Scottish artists 'seizing their place in a global market' or, as Mike Small puts it, 'culture-as-product'.[21] Again, that elitist, snobbish attitude comes to the fore. The very idea that artists might make money from what they do is obviously anathema, while popularity demeans any such work. Appealing to *hoi polloi* is tantamount to prostitution; much better to just have your work appreciated by a tiny clique. Small's snootiness even extends to his website; about which he is precious to the point of pettiness.

Bampots Utd is a blog, run by a guy called Mick (I don't know his surname), which is an eclectic mix of football, other sports, politics and anything else that Mick thinks might interest his readers. He writes himself now and again, and provides a forum for others to discuss practically everything; mostly, however, Mick trawls the internet to find interesting, often new blogs, which he re-blogs on his own site. This re-blogging, though, never amounts to wholesale theft. Mick provides the initial few paragraphs and then a link to the original, to which anyone that wants to read the rest has to go.

Anybody that writes, whether it be stories, poems or blogs, wants others to read their work. Without readers, one might as well just keep a diary, to be burned at the time of one's death. Mick has promoted all manner of blogs, about different topics from rugby to healthy living.[22] One of the blogs he promoted in the past was my own, for which I am eternally grateful. He helped to increase my readership tenfold and continues to promote my blog and my books. I am probably not the only one that has Mick to thank for the number of hits on their blog. You would imagine that anyone would be grateful for what essentially amounts to free advertising. You would, rather perversely, be wrong.

In March 2015, as he had done many times before, Mick re-blogged an article that appeared on Bella Caledonia. The character that had written the piece accused Mick of 'copyright infringement'; a ridiculous position to take. And then Mike Small, rather pretentiously calling himself the 'editor' of Bella Caledonia, got involved, also accusing Mick of stealing other people's stuff. When Mick asked Small for evidence, he was blocked and barred from Bella Caledonia.[23]

You might notice my name cropping up in the comments. This was referring to the time I sent two books to Mike Small. I had written on Bella Caledonia's book page, asking if he would review my books. He agreed, as long as a I sent paperback copies, which I duly did. After months with no sign of a review and no answer to my posts on Bella Caledonia, I practically had to shame Small into returning my books. At first, he claimed not to have received them and then, lo and behold, he returned one of them, saying that he had lost the other. How he had managed to lose something he had never received was not explained.

Small did, to be honest, offer to pay for the lost book.

Instead, I asked him just to give my book a mention on his website and perhaps provide a link. That was the last I heard from him and he never did mention my book. Perhaps I should have called it 'Son of Lanark' and he would have been all over it!

Obviously, Small does not want us ignorant scum participating on his website. Instead, we have just to wait until he and his elitist cronies tell us which party to vote for and then go and do it. Tugging of the forelock is, of course, entirely at one's own discretion.

In Scottish Labour leaders may come and leaders may go but there seems always to be one particular personality at the forefront of getting digs in at the Scottish Government; Jackie Baillie. No matter what the argument, there is Baillie, right forefinger jabbing while, in her left hand, she brandishes a piece of paper. Any outsider looking on would be forgiven for thinking that Baillie was in charge of the opposition at Holyrood.

In fact, Baillie has never stood for the party leadership. This might well have to do with her privileged background. She was born in Hong Kong and educated at Windermere St Mary's School in the Lake District, where fees are more than double those of most other public schools. When there was speculation in 2011 that Baillie might actually stand for the leadership, one senior Labour source said, 'Jackie Baillie is a very able politician but she has an 'accent problem' that could damage her campaign.'[24]

It is rather unfortunate that your background can hold back your political career but that is the position we are in nowadays, where image is everything. All political parties employ PR companies these days, who pander to people's prejudices. If you are too fat, too thin, are bald or have a beard, then you might as well give up before you start. One professor of politics was surprised at Baillie's background being an issue, saying, 'Labour has a good tradition of promoting people with public school backgrounds. It didn't stop Tony Blair and it hasn't stopped Harriet Harman.'[25] This, however, betrays a rather naïve ignorance of modern politics.

Tony Blair's success as Labour leader was entirely down

to the fact that he looked like a Tory and spoke like a Tory; something that was calculated to appeal to the English voter. Scots in general do not like folk that put on airs and graces (unless you happen to be a contributor to Bella Caledonia) and have a distrust of posh voices. Whether that is fair or not is beside the point; it happens to be one of the prejudices that many Scots have. With a posh, English accent, Baillie would find it difficult to win elections in Scotland; in just the same way as a working-class Scottish voice would be a severe handicap in English politics.

Still, Baillie's accent has never kept her quiet at all; she always seems to have plenty to say. Have a look at the chamber proceedings in the Scottish Parliament and you will see that her right forefinger gets a workout practically every day.[26]

Perhaps her ambitions lie in England, since her position on Trident is totally at odds with the general feeling in Scotland. She was the only Labour MSP to vote against the Scottish Government proposal to scrap Trident,[27] which is completely in tune with many Labour Westminster MPs, who oppose their leader's stance on nuclear disarmament. Baillie explained her decision to vote as she did: 'Whilst I respect the position of unilateralists, I don't believe that action alone will trigger other nations to reduce their weapons.'[28] That sounded straight from the Blairite, Little Englander handbook.

Baillie also went on to express concerns about job losses at Faslane. Job losses were a common theme with Baillie, who, along with the others in her party, blamed the Scottish Government for any increase in unemployment figures. The story, especially from Jackie Baillie, was that the SNP had been constantly lying to the Scottish people:

> Never again should the people of Scotland be misled about the future of our country. We need more transparency and responsibility, so the people of Scotland can trust what they are being told. The SNP promised a second oil boom, and produced some dodgy figures to make their case. The worrying events of recent days make it clear that their claim just wasn't

true. Our oil workers, and all Scots, deserve better. This is after all about jobs.[29]

Her solution was the setting up of a Scottish Office for Budget Responsibility, but with a far wider remit than its UK counterpart. Baillie was suggesting that the new body should scrutinise each party's election manifesto to check their credibility.[30] Of course, such a scheme is open to abuse and we saw, during the Independence Referendum, how so-called independent bodies are, in fact, usually linked, directly or indirectly, to government. Also, it was rather strange that Baillie and her party should be calling for such an organisation when Labour looked all but finished in Scotland. Why did they not want an Office of Budget Responsibility when they were in power?

Baillie was not the only one that accused the SNP of lying during the Referendum campaign; it had been a common theme in the media ever since the NO majority was declared. In 2016 this accusation was still being bandied about, especially in March, when it was time for the GERS figures to be released.

13
GER-ymandering?

'Bullet. Dodged. #GERS'[1] This was the reaction on Twitter of Ruth Davidson to the GERS figures issued on 9th March 2016. GERS stands for Government Expenditure and Revenue Scotland and is 'compiled by statisticians and economists in the Office of the Chief Economic Adviser of the Scottish Government.'[2] The Daily Record used one of their usual, dreadful puns: 'The Great Eckscape'.[3] (A ten-year-old could have come up with something better.) All-in-all it appeared to be a day for gloating; if you happened to be a Unionist, that was.

The figures showed that Scotland had a deficit of nearly £15bn, or, as the BBC gleefully pointed out, around 10% of Scotland's output, more than double the level for the whole UK or a £1,400 overspend per head compared to the UK.[4] It certainly seemed to be a damning indictment of the Scottish Government and appeared to make it plain that independence would never have worked. Unionist politicians even went as far as to say that the SNP had lied in its White Paper during the Independence Referendum.[5]

In fact, the SNP were not the only ones that had expected an upturn in the price of oil. It was not long after the Independence Referendum that the UK Government awarded 134 new licences to drill in offshore fields; one of the biggest awards of licences since they began in 1964.[6] Such an action showed that it was obvious that the UK Government, and the oil industry for that matter, believed that the price per barrel was going to increase. Since both the

UK Government and the oil industry expected the price of oil to go back up, it was entirely reasonable for the SNP to assume the same. There were no lies involved and nobody was trying to con the electorate.

The GERS figures are compiled by economists and statisticians; something which does not necessarily fill one with confidence. Statistics is not just about crunching numbers; it is about the method used and how the resulting figures are presented. Even at its most basic level, Statistics is all smoke and mirrors, as I used to tell my primary-school pupils.

Have a look at the two bar charts below. They are not based on any particular figures; I have just used the template chart provided by Microsoft Word.

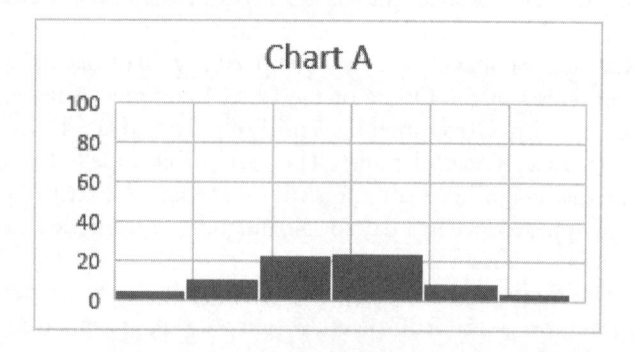

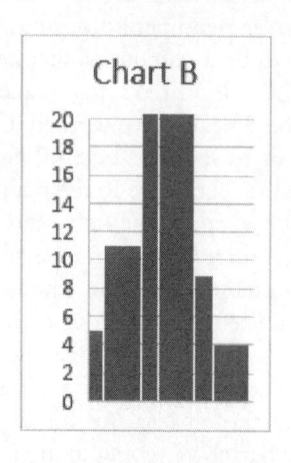

As you can see, in Chart A there is not much of a difference between the fourth bar and the sixth one. In Chart B, however, the difference between the two bars is huge. And, yet, both show exactly the same thing. A change in the vertical axis, making the numbers go up in different stages, as well as the simple expedient of reducing the size of the horizontal axis, changes the whole complexion of the figures.

And that is not the only way that statistics can be presented to show what you want to show. We all remember learning at school about 'means' 'modes' and 'medians' and the different results gained by using each method of working out an average. And that is just the simple stuff; who knows what else statistical experts get up to?

Then there are the economists. The one thing economists have in common with the rest of us is that while we do not know what they are on about, neither do they. You never hear economists explaining to us what is going to happen; they are good, however, at telling us why things *have* happened. For all the good it does anyone after the event!

Economists are like the experts you get presenting horse racing on television. Once the race is over they are full of how the winner was obvious, given its pedigree, form and the condition of the ground. If they had told us all that *before* the race, then it might have been of some use. Equally, an economist telling why a recession *has* happened is about as useful as a chocolate fireguard.

Things get even worse when economists come up with theories and disastrous when politicians follow such theories. The orthodox belief in the years up to the Second World War said that inflation had to be kept in check, even if it led to mass unemployment. In fact, large-scale unemployment was held to be good for the economy since it helped keep wages down. After the war Keynesian ideas took over, believing in the opposite of the Deflationists. Full employment, or as near to it as possible, was actually a cure for inflation and would keep it in check.

From the mid-1970s something strange began to happen; both unemployment and inflation were rising. Economists, just like politicians, were puzzled; it was something that was supposed to be impossible. Then along came Monetarism, essentially just Deflation in disguise, with the concomitant rise in unemployment. Luckily for Thatcher, there was all the revenue from North Sea oil to help cover up the Government's follies.

Nowadays the only economic policy that appears to be being followed is keeping the banks afloat, even if that means cuts in public spending and poverty and misery for millions. Along with this worship of banks is the encouragement of so-called 'wealth providers' with lower taxes. These characters and companies, however, find ways to dodge paying even the small amounts of tax required of them, while they outsource production to foreign slave-labour sweatshops and bind employees in the UK to zero-hours contracts. In reality, the only wealth these people provide all goes into their own pockets.

As well as treating anything produced by a statistician or an economist with suspicion, there is also the fact that the GERS figures show how Scotland is performing within the United Kingdom. Who is to say, with different priorities and policies, that the exact same figures would result if Scotland were to be independent? All the figures show is that the status quo is not working.

It has to be admitted, though, that supporters of Scottish independence have not been above using the GERS figures when it suited them. In previous years, they were happy to point to the figures as proof that Scotland would manage fine if it were independent.[7] But it was equally the case that opponents of independence claimed that the figures were evidence of how well Scotland fared within the UK.[8]

Now that the figures are not so great opinions on them have reversed. Nicola Sturgeon was defiant, saying that the figures merely reflected the global crisis of the price of oil; apart from that, Scotland's economy 'has remained resilient with record levels of employment, positive economic growth and growing exports.'[9] The Unionist parties, on the other hand, were cock-a-hoop, gloating like schoolchildren.[10] 'Thank God we voted NO!' was the general consensus.

Kevin McKenna, in the Guardian, had an important point to make about the GERS figures; one that the Unionists would not like.

Nowhere in the so-called analysis was it pointed out that these figures are for a single year; that economic forecast is better conducted over 10 years; that Scotland's economy over the last 10 years has been robust and that they are, as Dr Neil McGarvey of Strathclyde University's School of Government and Public Policy pointed out, "by no means definitive measurements of what Scotland's public accounts would look like".[11]

Alex Massie, in the Spectator, had something even more hard-hitting to say:

Unionists minded to crow today as the Scottish government publishes figures that are, frankly, ruinous should remember that by doing so they are playing the nationalists at their own game. That is, if inconvenient, even disagreeable, economic news demolishes the argument for independence then it stands to follow that healthier economic figures, such as those projected with such heroic optimism during the referendum campaign, make a strong case for that independence.[12]

Nobody on the Unionist side, however, was prepared to heed what Massie was saying; they were too busy gloating. No doubt if Scotland's economy picked up they would all be ready again to put it down to being a part of the UK. Whatever the truth of the matter, there was one thing that nobody on either side mentioned; what actually constituted expenditure in the GERS report?

The report was not just concerned with expenditure by the Scottish Government but also with spending by the UK Government for the benefit of Scottish residents. The biggest individual item of expenditure was classed as Social Protection. This included social security benefits and amounted to almost £23bn. The next largest was Health, which swallowed up more than £11.5bn. These two together made up just over half of the total expenditure.[13]

It is difficult to find up-to-date figures but in 2012, more than 90% of new housing-benefit claims in the UK were made by people in employment.[14] Probably not a lot has changed in the last few years. The Mail, the Telegraph and the Express all scream about generations of skivers and evil immigrants all bleeding the taxpayer dry, but the fact is that most DWP benefits, leaving pensions aside, are paid to people in work and the long-term sick. In fact, in 2013 Jobseekers allowance accounted for only a small portion of benefits spending.[15]

DWP quarterly statistics in February 2016 showed a decline in the amount of people in the UK claiming Jobseekers Allowance, while money paid out for Employment Support Allowance, disability benefits and carers allowances were on the increase.[16] Although the figures are somewhat skewed by the rolling-out of the new Universal Credit, it is still clear that the amount of people on sickness benefits is definitely increasing.

In Scotland one of the major problems faced by the NHS is mental illness. Scottish Government estimates put the number of people suffering from mental illness in any one year as high as a third of the population.[17] This includes dementia patients and, rather distressingly, children with severe mental-health problems.[18] Among those of working age, however, the biggest problem appears to be depression, with the number of people being prescribed anti-depression drugs increasing year on year.[19]

Studies have shown that mental-health problems, including depression, anxiety, alcohol and drug abuse and even schizophrenia, are linked to poverty and deprivation.[20] The NHS, and other agencies, are having to spend a fortune tackling these problems, which are essentially a side-effect of the large-scale poverty found in most towns and cities in Scotland.

Much of the expenditure outlined in the GERS figures, then, is caused by low pay having to be topped-up with benefits and mental-health issues due to poverty and deprivation. Both of these issues are directly linked to the policies of the Government in Westminster. Allowing employers to get away with paying what in many cases amounts to less than subsistence wages means extra expenditure for the DWP. This, in turn, leads to people being trapped in poverty, which, as we know means more incidence of mental-health problems. With such factors being in evidence since the 1980s, whole generations have grown up with poverty and mental-health problems being basically a way of life.

Tackling these problems is going to need a long-term strategy, which is virtually impossible as long as Scotland is tied to Westminster's London-centric political and economic policies. More powers for Holyrood might allow the Scottish Government to take more action on these fundamental issues, but it is going to be extremely difficult, as setting minimum standards of pay etc. are powers that are still retained, for the present at least, by Westminster. Throwing money at the problem, as Kezia Dugdale was suggesting, was not going to make a lot of difference, especially since the plans she was outlining could not be put into force until 2017 at the earliest; a fact that she disingenuously always failed to mention.[21]

A large chunk of the 'financial black hole' facing Scotland, then, was actually being caused by policies at Westminster; policies that Labour failed to tackle during its fourteen-year tenure of office. It is one of the ridiculous ironies of our society that employers are allowed to pay low wages, and subsequently take on more staff, that helps to improve employment figures while, at the same time, costing the taxpayer a fortune. It is equally ironic that increased expenditure caused by Westminster's policies is then laid at the door of the Scottish Government as proof positive that Scottish independence is a non-starter.

Alex Massie's article in the Spectator had another uncomfortable truth to point out to those opposed to Scottish independence; nationalism does not depend on cold, hard economics.

> …while the Yes campaign undoubtedly needed a veneer of economic plausibility its strongest arguments never depended on anything so mundane as mere numbers. It was, instead, an argument built on identity and the twin senses of self and place. That argument still stands.[22]

Massie was correct in his assertion that economics was a secondary consideration in the campaign for Scottish independence. He was, however, wrong in stressing the importance of identity, self and place. Such arguments are redolent of the *Blut und Boden* policies of Nazi Germany; an accusation that opponents of independence threw at nationalists during the Referendum, but which was completely untrue. Nor did the more left-wing aspects of the Scottish independence campaign constitute any kind of Nazi-like *Volksgemeinschaft*. The independent Scotland envisaged by the SNP, and others, was all-inclusive and, indeed, was ready to welcome immigrants. Opponents found this nearly impossible to understand.

Ironically, many of those that had accused Scottish independence campaigners of being anti-English fascists were using the very arguments they had purported to hate in their crusade to leave the European Union. A quick Google search throws up what the campaign to leave the EU was all about in England; xenophobia and racism. All the rhetoric was about halting immigration and the danger of allowing potential terrorists into the UK. Meanwhile, the campaign to stay in concentrated on economic arguments. It was all very familiar.

The EU Referendum was practically a re-run of the independence one, except this time the xenophobia and racism of those wanting to leave was real, rather than in the imaginations of opponents. Just as in the Independence Referendum, there were even those in Europe saying about the UK, 'Let them leave if they want', while resentment was building up, particularly in France, about concessions being granted to Britain.[23] Of course, the replies to this from English Euro-sceptics were predictably chauvinistic.

I have never liked the French they wissed (sic) off and left our soldiers on the dunkirk (sic) beach they are an arrogant nation it shows in their manners they have bad breath and stink of garlic we had to rescue them twice from the clutches of Germany they resent this thier (sic) soldiers are surrender monkeys.[24]

The whole campaign to leave the EU could probably be summed up in those few lines; utter contempt for foreigners intermingled with a one-sided view of history. There would be plenty of French folk ready to point out that it was Britain that betrayed France in 1940. Treaty obligations between the two countries were all about mutual defence; it was Britain that ran off and left France to the Nazis. But when did uncomfortable facts ever get in the way of a right-winger's argument?

Interestingly, Nicola Sturgeon was well aware of the similarities of the two campaigns. Even before the EU Referendum campaign started, she warned that another 'Project Fear' would actually put people off voting to stay in Europe and called for a positive campaign.[25] She also reiterated the warning that if Scotland voted to stay in the EU, while England voted to leave, then another independence referendum would be triggered.[26]

The answer from Unionists to this suggestion was that the SNP had claimed that the referendum of 2014 was a 'once in a generation event'.[27] John Swinney, however, was ready with a counter-argument. His contention was that Scotland might possibly be betrayed in the upcoming EU Referendum. He said that the Unionists had made it plain, during the Scottish Independence Referendum, that an independent Scotland would no longer be a part of the EU and that staying in the UK would be the only way for it to remain in the EU. Now the UK Government was threatening that Scotland might be dragged, against its will, out of the EU.

Swinney voiced this argument on the BBC's Question Time on 10th March 2016. This particular programme resulted in storms of protest and it is worth looking at what actually occurred in detail.

14
On The QT

When John Swinney was explaining how the Unionists had lied to Scotland over the EU, he was interrupted by David Dimbleby. The presenter said that everyone had been well aware that there was going to be a referendum on the EU before the Scottish Independence campaign took place. This was a disingenuous argument since nobody could possibly have been sure that the Tories were going to win the upcoming General Election. All polls were pointing to a hung parliament, which could well have meant that there would be no referendum on the EU at all.

When Swinney attempted to argue the point, Dimbleby spoke over him. It was not the first time during the programme that Swinney was rudely interrupted and not allowed to finish what he was saying; unfortunately, it was not the last either.

Question Time that night, 10th March 2016, came from Dundee. It was the day after the GERS figures had been released so it was to be expected that it would perhaps be a bad-tempered programme. With an audience representative of the city, partisanship over politics could result in furious arguments over the GERS figures. It did not, however, turn out that way.

During the course of the programme, twenty members of the audience spoke, either asking questions or being invited to comment. Of those twenty, eleven of them happened to be English. Now, there is nothing wrong with English people speaking on a programme being broadcast from Scotland; after all, plenty of English folk have moved to Scotland and are as entitled as anyone else to have their say. It is extremely doubtful, however, that over half the population of Dundee is English, so the people invited to speak were hardly representative.

Then again, perhaps this is being a trifle unfair. Maybe the
rest of the audience had submitted rather anodyne or ridiculous questions, leaving little choice in who would be chosen to speak. That, however, does not explain why most of those asked to comment, seemingly at random, turned out to be English. If people were chosen at random to comment, then it means that the majority of the audience was most likely composed of English people. If that was not the case, then it meant that those chosen to comment were hand-picked beforehand. Either way it betrayed a distinct bias on the part of the BBC.

There were, of course, immediate complaints about this bias. 'Twitter is very confused that everyone in Dundee has an English accent #bbcqt' and 'I know Dundee. This is a very odd Dundee audience. #bbcqt' were just two of the comments on the Question Time Twitter account.[1] The BBC was outraged:

> Question Time audiences are always selected in accordance with our guidelines on fairness and impartiality, and this week was no different.
> We are careful to select audiences which are politically balanced and reflect a range of political views.
> Every member of this audience was a Scottish resident and from Dundee or the surrounding area.[2]

Nobody, however, was convinced. It seemed as if the BBC considered the surrounding area of Dundee to stretch all the way to London. There were complaints galore, not only to the BBC directly, but on Twitter and newspaper forums as well. The most interesting complaints came from people that had actually been in the Question Time audience. One person had this to say:

> Some of them were from Glasgow, Edinburgh and Aberdeen. How local is that, do you think? I heard them discuss their travel arrangements. The audience may have been evenly spread, but the questions were clearly carefully chosen and those selected to make comments were eerily one-sided. I had my hand up to speak a huge amount of the time and no one came near me.[3]

And that was not the only thing that was noticed about the audience; there just happened to be two Labour members, who had stood in the 2015 General Election, in the audience as well.[4] Braden Davy had moved from his home in Northumbria to Aberdeen in 2012 and was chosen as the Labour candidate for Gordon. Unfortunately for him, it was the same constituency that Alex Salmond chose to stand in. Also unfortunately, young Mr Davy seemed a rather mixed-up character, who did not know where he stood on anything.[5] This was what probably led to his reluctance to answer questions; he tended to ban folk that asked anything on his Facebook page.[6]

Such a tyro did not stand a chance against a political heavyweight like Salmond. Perhaps the idea was to give him some experience in elections before finding him a safer constituency to stand in. As things turned out, there was no such thing as a safe Labour seat in Scotland anymore. The tsunami of SNP votes swept all before it, not just Davis.

On Question Time, young Davis was one of the ones 'chosen at random' to offer a comment. He went into a lengthy tirade about the EU and why the UK, and Scotland with it, should leave. No doubt we shall hear of Mr Davis again; probably standing for UKIP in the south of England.

A more sinister member of the audience was a woman that introduced herself as Kathy Aliberti. She had a question to ask, which was all about the GERS figures and how the SNP had 'lied' during the Independence Referendum. Many people recognised her immediately; but they knew her as Kathy Wiles, Labour candidate for Angus in the 2015

General Election.[7]

Wiles was chosen at the end of June 2014; nearly a year before the General Election was due to take place.[8] Only a matter of days after her candidacy was announced, Wiles was forced to resign after likening some children, who took part with their parents in a demonstration outside BBC Scotland headquarters in Glasgow over bias in the Independence campaign, to the Hitler Youth.[9] She even put an illustration of the Nazi organisation on Twitter to ram home her point, comparing it with an original photograph of the children in Glasgow. This, understandably, caused outrage. Apologising unreservedly, Wiles said, 'My intention was to make a point about the dangers of using young children in political campaigns, not to make any inference about those in the photo.'[10]

Obviously, Wiles was not the brightest light on the Christmas tree and she had let her hatred of the SNP get the better of her. Apparently, the woman has two university degrees and worked as an expert in learning and teaching;[11] yet she does not seem to know the difference between 'infer' and 'imply'. It was probably just as well that she resigned when she did, before getting the chance to do something worse.

As Stu Campbell pointed out, Wiles had been rather a strange choice in the first place.[12] She had previously shown a remarkable ability to open her mouth and put her foot straight in it. Some of the things she had posted on the internet, prior to being selected, bordered on the xenophobic or even racist.

In 2013 Wiles complained about the eligibility rules for voting in the forthcoming Independence Referendum.[13] She moaned about people 'with temporary residency' being allowed to vote while 'born Scots with Scottish property and interests' were not. She whined about a 'tiny minority' that could 'disenfranchise' her from her 'nationality forever'. Obviously, nobody in the Labour Party had bothered to look into the woman's background.

To be fair to Wiles, she probably is not racist; she was just letting her hatred of the SNP cloud her judgment once again. If the electorate had included Scots living abroad, or in the rest of the UK, and excluded foreigners actually resident in Scotland, Wiles would have been equally as scathing about that. The old *Blut und Boden* argument would have been trotted out to, once again, make the SNP look like Nazis. Wiles's problem, like others in the Labour Party, was hatred of the SNP, rather than hatred of foreigners.

At any rate, it was strange to say the least that this ridiculous woman and her bewildered colleague managed to wheedle their way onto Question Time. Were they acting independently, or with the connivance of Scottish Labour? If it was the latter, then it was a remarkable own goal. It certainly betrayed the bias of the BBC in letting these two politicians *manqués* onto the programme.

It seemed that they were not the only ones to have managed to sneak in. one Englishman had a point to make that was totally at odds with the mood of the programme. He said he had jumped at the opportunity to move to Scotland because he found what was happening here exciting. Coming from the Lake District, the gentleman professed to be sick and tired of the London-centrism of the Westminster Government. He was all in favour of Scottish independence, which surely should have excluded him from commenting. He looked like a wily, old goat so he had probably claimed to be a Tory Euro-sceptic to get on the programme. His comments came as a breath of fresh air in an atmosphere of bias and bile.

This Englishman could be seen laughing when one of the panel, Tim Stanley of the Telegraph, said that the UK was all about the richer parts helping out those areas that were struggling. It was a ridiculous claim to make in Scotland of all places. Westminster had bled Scotland dry and spent all the cash on London, ignoring abject poverty in the rest of the United Kingdom. And it was still going on, with the Tory Government attacking the poor, sick and disabled to benefit the money men in the capital. All Stanley managed to prove was that he was completely out of touch with what was going on outside his London bubble.

Stanley's inclusion on the panel also showed how out of touch the BBC was. In fact, the composition of the whole panel was indicative of the BBC's failure to understand how politics had changed in Scotland. As well as the Telegraph journalist, there were Ruth Davidson, John Swinney, Labour MSP Jenny Marra, Liberal-Democrat MSP Willie Rennie and Green Party MSP Patrick Harvie.[14]

When Question Time takes place anywhere in England, the party-political aspect of the panel, and even the audience can result in some spectacular disagreements and even heated arguments. Labour will be against Tory, while Lib-Dem will try to attack both equally, trying to forget its own participation in the coalition Government. There is usually a Green Party, a UKIP member, a journalist or a famous personality thrown into the mix as well. Now that we have a Tory Government in power, watching Question Time is sometimes like going back in time to the 1980s, with well-worn arguments being employed. You can often guess what each panel member is going to say before he or she opens their mouth. The situation in Scotland, however, has changed radically.

Going down the party-political road, as was done in Dundee, effectively means a member of the SNP with everyone else on the panel against him. John Swinney had to hold his own against four political opponents, who, despite being in different parties, were united against the Scottish Government. The only potential ally available to Swinney was Patrick Harvie, who, as a Green Party member, had his own agenda.

The make-up of the audience probably reflected party politics as well, skewing it in favour of Unionism and against the SNP. It might well be that the BBC was not demonstrating bias but ignorance and complete indifference, which is just as bad. With its London-centric focus, the Question Time backroom team obviously has no idea whatsoever of what is going on in Scotland. It is no longer about Labour versus Tory, with a bit of input from other parties, as it is in England. Politics has changed in Scotland; the BBC, however, has not moved with it.

That, however, does not explain or excuse the number of English voices we heard. Nor does it explain why the audience was apparently shipped in from other areas. The complaints about the programme produced a backlash, which showed either a remarkable lack of understanding or a cynical attempt to blacken the independence cause.

One newspaper cited the fact that Jenny Marra was a born-and-bred Dundonian as evidence that there had been no bias, while featuring a woman that had immigrated to Dundee from Australia, who complained that she had as much right to a voice as anyone.[15] This was a ridiculous argument, as the comments on the article show. The Australian woman said she felt welcome in Dundee and Scotland, 'But there is an element that makes me feel uncomfortable that says you're not Scottish unless you speak with a Scottish accent.'[16]

With all due respect to the woman, it was a rather stupid position to take. Nobody was complaining about English voices on Question Time *per se*; it was the paucity of Scottish voices that was the problem. Nobody ever suggested that non-Scots resident in Scotland should not have a voice; nobody apart from Kathy Wiles, that is! To have the programme completely dominated by such voices, however, meant that it was in no way representative. One cannot help wondering what the reaction would be if a Question Time audience in London was dominated by accents that were not indigenous to England.

15
Fear and Smear Redux

So there it was. While Scotland was voting for the SNP to run the Scottish Government and, overwhelmingly, to serve the country at Westminster, politicians and the media were working hard to undermine our elected representatives. The whole Establishment was running scared; the very idea of Scotland being independent filled it with dread.

Scotland had, for decades, been Westminster's cash-cow, allowing it to pay for ridiculous, Thatcherite policies and build up London as a financial centre. There were still plenty of natural resources still to be exploited and Westminster had deep pockets to be filled. The price of oil might have plummeted but it was already showing signs of recovery at the beginning of March 2016.[1] The smoke-and-mirrors economy of London needed a tangible commodity to back it, so Scotland was still going to be useful for the foreseeable future.

We saw during the Scottish Independence Referendum what dirty tricks the Establishment was willing to employ to hold onto Scotland's assets. Such tactics were still in evidence, since the *status quo* had been shaken to its very core with the mass support evident for the SNP. The whole idea of independence had to be stamped out, which meant undermining the Scottish Government and our SNP MPs at Westminster.

Like the pigs at the end of Animal Farm, Scottish Labour had become the Establishment in Scotland, in thrall to the party leadership in London. The UK party could elect as leader all the Jeremy Corbyns it liked; the fact was that the parliamentary party, as well as the top echelons, were still Blairite in composition. Scottish Labour is shackled to London and is not free to act on its own, having to keep one eye on what is happening in England and Wales. As many commentators have said, Scotland has moved on and left Scottish Labour behind.

While ostensibly opposing the Tory Westminster Government, Scottish Labour works hand-in-hand with the Tories in Scotland to attack the SNP. Every single thing the Scottish Government does is put under intense scrutiny and subjected to criticism, with no serious suggestions as to what should be done instead. Even the negotiations over the new powers for Holyrood saw the Scottish Government come under fire day-in, day-out, with very few fingers of blame pointing in the direction of Westminster.

The media in Scotland helps out as well, criticising the SNP and blaming it for everything from the near-collapse of the oil industry to the crisis in the NHS. Innuendo, the twisting of facts and downright lies are all used to attack the SNP. sometimes they like to highlight something the Scottish Government has done that they would never dream of criticising Westminster for.

'MSPs kept silent on human rights abuses while seeking £1.3bn for new hospitals and motorways from Qatar', said a Daily Record headline on 13th March 2016.[2] The story was all about how Holyrood Development Minister, Humza Yousaf, had gone to Qatar to seek investment and neglected to mention the human-rights abuses in the country. The Scottish Government pointed out that it had raised the issue of human rights on other occasions, but we were meant to ignore that.

As you might expect, it was a Labour MSP, Neil Findlay, whom we have met before, that obtained the damning information via a FOI request. Obviously, Scottish Labour was looking to muckraking tactics, rather than coming up with policies, to try to win votes in the Holyrood elections. The Daily Record, as usual, was there to lend a helping hand.

As was pointed out in the comments section,[3] there was no mention by the Record of Westminster's overtures to Qatar, under the Tories, the Coalition and Labour. These overtures were not just looking for investment; they were looking to sell arms, surely something much worse. And Qatar was not the only dodgy regime that Westminster courted. Tony Blair, Gordon Brown and David Cameron have all been pictured bowing and scraping to Saudi royalty, while Westminster has also lined up a deal for China to build, run and maintain nuclear power stations in the UK. Both these nations rank high on the list for human-rights abuses; yet there has been no word of condemnation in the Daily Record or anywhere else in the mainstream media. It seems that it is only reprehensible when the SNP does it.

And then came the 'Jaffa Cake' affair. Scottish Education Secretary, Angela Constance, mentioned on Twitter that she was packing her son's bag to go to school camp. Like other parents, she obviously has a bit of a soft centre when it comes to her offspring. She said:

> Been packing my weans bag 4 school camp & despite clear instructions from school..I just had to put in a packet of Jaffa Cakes...just had to[4]

Incredibly, she found herself immediately under attack from self-righteous individuals on Twitter, as well as some hypocritical finger-wagging by the Daily Record. Labour MSP Neil Findlay, meanwhile, said, 'Next she'll be shoving burgers through the school railings.'[5]

Ms Constance should really have said nothing about this. She probably thought that she was showing herself to be just another parent but, when it comes to the SNP, our media does not act in a normal fashion. The only real surprise in this massive overreaction was that, for once, Jackie Baillie had nothing to say on the matter.

The snack that was sneaked into the boy's bag was most likely one of those mini-packs of Jaffa Cakes; a far cry from my own experience of children going to school camp. One P4 boy had a huge rucksack and a large suitcase with him, which was a bit over the top for a stay of four nights. I soon discovered that the suitcase was filled to the brim with biscuits, crisps and sweets. Rather hilariously, there simply was not the time for him to eat any of this, so it all ended up going home with him. Constance Junior's Jaffa Cakes will probably come back unopened as well.

The episode showed how petty that attacks on the SNP could get. The Daily Record, and the people it quoted, were all howling about 'double standards' and 'setting a bad example'. In the grand scheme of things, however, it is hardly the crime of the century.

As well as having to contend with attacks from Scottish Labour and its cronies in the media, there arose a new body to have a go at the SNP; RISE. As we have seen, our media have not been backward in promoting this group in order to help split the independence vote. Meanwhile, the RISE candidates themselves are happy enough to reap the benefit of this promotion and are not above cynically trying to pander to certain sections of the electorate.

At the same time, other members and supporters of RISE are undermining the independence cause with their snooty, pseudo-intellectual espousal of a long-dead language. While inventing myths about 'Scots' being forcibly replaced with Standard English, they want to promote a 'Standard Scots' language. As we have seen, this undermines not only the case for independence but, indirectly, the SNP as well. Giving these people the benefit of the doubt means that their endeavours are misguided and ingenuous. It might well be the case, however, that there is a sinister cynicism behind it.

I have outlined in this book how the Scottish Government and our SNP MPs at Westminster have their jobs made all the more difficult by snide attacks from all quarters. Even when our media agrees with some measure introduced, or supported, by the SNP, whether in Holyrood or Westminster, it is always qualified with a 'but…'. Personal attacks on SNP MPs and MSPs have been unrelenting and apologies have been few and far between, or even non-existent, when the stories have been proven wrong.

It is to be hoped that the Scottish electorate is not taken in by all this subterfuge. I have seen one or two folk commenting on newspaper forums that they have voted SNP in the past but will not be doing so again. Whether these comments are genuine or the work of some Unionist with an agenda is uncertain. What is certain is that the Establishment, both Left and Right, in Scotland and in England, are terrified of the prospect of Scottish independence. The dirty tricks employed to prevent it happening have been ongoing ever since the Independence Referendum was first announced.

Hopefully, all these underhand shenanigans have been in vain. If this book contributes, even in a small way, to undermining the dirty work of the Establishment, then writing it will have been a worthwhile exercise.

NOTES

Introduction

[1] https://www.sundaypost.com/news/scottish-news/poll-expert-claims-snp-are-set-to-win-45-seats/
[2] http://www.heraldscotland.com/news/13212501.Brown__SNP_votes_let_the_Tories_in/
[3] http://www.thedrum.com/news/2015/03/09/conservatives-belittle-ed-miliband-latest-attack-ad
[4] http://www.thedrum.com/news/2015/04/19/conservative-poster-shows-snp-head-nicola-sturgeon-playing-puppet-mastered-miliband
[5] http://www.mirror.co.uk/news/uk-news/labour-not-fight-dirty-election-5082013
[6] http://www.dailyrecord.co.uk/news/politics/general-election-2015-jim-murphy-5637727#GfC7jiAXxqZfAXUY.97
[7] http://www.independent.co.uk/news/uk/politics/snp-leader-alex-salmond-faces-referendum-rethink-as-sun-sets-on-alliance-with-rupert-murdochs-news-8556199.html
[8] http://www.bbc.co.uk/news/election-2015-scotland-32523804
[9] ibid
[10] http://www.pressgazette.co.uk/sunday-herald-reports-doubling-circulation-after-lone-stand-favour-independence
[11] http://www.bbc.co.uk/news/uk-scotland-scotland-business-26366464
[12] https://en.wikipedia.org/wiki/List_of_newspapers_in_the_United_Kingdom_by_circulation (It is worth noting that Wikipedia uses figures from the Audit Bureau of Circulations; figures that are pretty accurate.)
[13] http://www.theguardian.com/commentisfree/2014/may/02/scottish-press-decline-hold-independent-scotland-to-account
[14] Pat Anderson: Fear and Smear – The Campaign Against Scottish Independence Chapter 4
[15] http://www.improvementservice.org.uk/east-ayrshire.html
[16] http://www.eastrenfrewshire.gov.uk/councillors-democracy
[17] http://www.edinburgh.gov.uk/info/20031/councillors_and_committees/298/make_up_of_the_council
[18] http://www.eastlothiancourier.com/news/

13557248.Tories_can_tip_the_scales_in_balance_of_power_for_control_of_East_Lothian/ The 'Comments' section reveals what the local issues were.

[19] http://www.bbc.co.uk/news/election/2015/results/england
[20] http://www.1001portails.com/itv_com_news_index_rss-t-54052-35412015-revealed_secret_labour_report_published_in_full.html#.Vqxp6pXctjp
[21] http://www.bbc.co.uk/news/election/2015/results/scotland
[22] http://www.ukpolitical.info/Turnout45.htm
[23] http://news.bbc.co.uk/1/shared/election2010/results/region/7.stm
[24] http://www.bbc.co.uk/news/election/2015/results/scotland
[25] http://news.bbc.co.uk/1/shared/election2010/results/region/7.stm
[26] http://www.theguardian.com/society/2002/feb/18/socialexclusion
[27] https://www.ipsosmori.com/researchpublications/researcharchive/3575/How-Britain-voted-in-2015.aspx?view=wide
[28] http://www.ukpolitical.info/Turnout15.htm
[29] http://www.dailyrecord.co.uk/news/politics/independence-referendum-figures-revealed-majority-5408163#rlabs=42%20p$6#F3yLFx0LXWd52Jjo.97
[30] http://www.bbc.co.uk/news/events/scotland-decides/results
[31] http://www.dailyrecord.co.uk/news/politics/independence-referendum-figures-revealed-majority-5408163#rlabs=42%20p$6#F3yLFx0LXWd52Jjo.97
[32] http://www.bbc.co.uk/news/election/2015/results/england

Chapter 1

[1] http://www.dailyrecord.co.uk/news/scottish-news/bosses-62bn-warship-torpedo-scots-5655855#3CxXvBD3OyePEF2U.97

[2] http://www.dailyrecord.co.uk/news/scottish-news/protest-staged-rosyth-over-claims-7266079#stoDdZU5ASgmBaoV.97

[3] ibid

[4] http://www.telegraph.co.uk/news/politics/conservative/10655849/Cabinets-warning-to-Scotland-over-North-Sea-oil.html

[5] ibid

[6] http://www.economist.com/blogs/economist-explains/2014/12/economist-explains-4

[7] http://news.stv.tv/scotland-decides/309795-scotland-would-now-be-bankrupt-lord-foulkes-tells-house-of-lords/

[8] https://www.epmag.com/battle-ahead-uk-north-sea-837016

[9] http://www.ibtimes.co.uk/centrica-ceo-osborne-should-cut-taxes-oil-producers-avoid-north-sea-field-closures-1541173

[10] http://www.upi.com/Business_News/Energy-Industry/2016/01/27/Scotland-wants-tax-support-for-North-Sea-energy/9641453895071/

[11] http://www.dailyrecord.co.uk/news/politics/nicola-sturgeon-told-quit-blame-7239425#WEwCVi0gIEymeIwm.97

[12] ibid

[13] http://www.dailyrecord.co.uk/news/politics/record-view-ditch-cheap-shots-7268261#PZ5QhXmYrvswERak.97

[14] http://www.theguardian.com/society/2014/jun/28/nhs-funding-crisis-general-election

[15] http://www.dailyrecord.co.uk/news/politics/nhs-staff-scotland-breaking-point-7267390#WDM0h74QhbXjvxJi.97

[16] http://www.theguardian.com/society/2015/jan/17/nurses-nhs-stress-leave-staff-breaking-point

[17] ibid

[18] http://weownit.org.uk/evidence/nhs

[19] http://www.express.co.uk/scotland/638290/GPs-blast-SNP-over-health-care-in-black-day-for-Nicola-Sturgeon

[20] ibid

[21] http://www.dailyrecord.co.uk/news/scottish-news/top-doctor-blasts-snp-lack-7252383#Mbs2lfQte0cMM76V.97

[22] ibid

[23] http://www.bma.org.uk/support-at-work/pay-fees-allowances/pay-scales/general-practitioners-pay

[24] http://www.thestudentroom.co.uk/showthread.php? t=968179
[25] ibid
[26] http://www.bma.org.uk/support-at-work/pay-fees-allowances/pay-scales/juniors-pay-scotland
[27] http://www.eis.org.uk/Pay_and_Conditions_of_Service/salary_scales.htm
[28] http://blog.oup.com/2012/07/how-to-become-a-doctor-uk/
[29] http://www.dailyrecord.co.uk/news/health/failures-nhs-killing-six-patients-7273017#W6AsqZ6yU5YH4wso.97
[30] http://www.bbc.co.uk/news/uk-scotland-scotland-politics-35548744
[31] http://www.dailyrecord.co.uk/news/health/failures-nhs-killing-six-patients-7273017#W6AsqZ6yU5YH4wso.97
[32] ibid
[33] http://news.stv.tv/east-central/259736-doctor-accuses-nhs-lothian-of-gagging-her-over-whistleblowing/
[34] ibid
[35] http://www.independent.co.uk/news/uk/politics/ceo-of-major-midlands-nhs-trust-quits-after-pressure-from-health-regulator-9854532.html
[36] http://www.independent.co.uk/life-style/health-and-families/health-news/locum-doctors-and-nurses-rip-off-nhs-says-health-services-regulator-a6862451.html
[37] http://www.bma.org.uk/news-views-analysis/news/2014/november/nhs-staring-into-the-abyss-says-bma
[38] http://search.aol.co.uk/aol/search?s_it=topsearchbox.search&s_chn=hp&v_t=aolukhomePage50.a&q=labour+call+for+end+to+free+university+education+in+scotland
[39] http://www.dailyrecord.co.uk/news/politics/kezia-dugdale-snp-cuts-education 7283528#rlabs=3%20rt$category%20p$6#l0IBKx1EgyWy9dQK.97
[40] http://news.scotland.gov.uk/News/Council-tax-freeze-continues-98b.aspx
[41] http://news.stv.tv/politics/108267-new-single-police-force-and-single-fire-service-to-be-created/
[42] http://www.theguardian.com/politics/2009/feb/11/alex-salmond-snp-local-income-tax
[43] ibid

[44] http://www.eveningtimes.co.uk/news/14247479.SNP_challenged_to_back_Labour_s_tax_rise_plan_to_avoid_cuts/
[45] ibid
[46] http://www.bbc.co.uk/news/uk-scotland-scotland-politics-34326185
[47] http://www.theguardian.com/politics/2015/mar/05/scottish-councils-pile-up-record-debt
[48] ibid
[49] http://www.bbc.co.uk/news/uk-scotland-14995385
[50] https://en.wikipedia.org/wiki/Lender_option_borrower_option
[51] http://www.bbc.co.uk/news/uk-scotland-33615619
[52] http://www.dailyrecord.co.uk/news/scottish-news/star-wars-scots-who-won-7118459#yrqcplVg2Sz6tEyR.97
[53] http://www.dailyrecord.co.uk/news/scottish-news/scotland-could-miss-out-biggest-7391484#eoUSWi7vlbkbduUp.97
[54] http://www.telegraph.co.uk/news/weather/12090049/Nicola-Sturgeon-urged-to-help-flood-victims-amid-calls-for-emergency-statement-in-parliament.html
[55] http://www.itv.com/news/2016-01-09/sturgeon-announces-12m-of-funding-to-help-scottish-flood-victims/
[56] https://www.sundaypost.com/news/political-news/snp-accused-of-taking-credit-for-flooding-funding-provided-by-uk-government/
[57] https://www.sundaypost.com/inside-the-sunday-edition/flood-victims-in-scotland-will-get-1k-more-each-than-flood-hit-english/

Chapter 2

[1] http://www.theguardian.com/politics/2014/sep/30/gordon-brown-david-cameron-scotland-trap

[2] http://www.bbc.co.uk/news/election-2015-32441969

[3] http://www.bbc.co.uk/news/uk-politics-34599998

[4] http://www.dailymail.co.uk/debate/article-2763744/I-demand-shamefully-unfair-Barnett-Formula-scrapped-LORD-BARNETT-architect-hated-subsidy-Scotland.html

[5] https://www.eveningexpress.co.uk/pipe/news/scotland/evel-may-mean-end-of-barnett-formula/

[6] http://www.bbc.co.uk/news/uk-scotland-scotland-politics-29213418

[7] http://www.dailyrecord.co.uk/news/politics/record-view-party-grievance-should-6763445#oXwRycHIx3WKUhbW.97

[8] http://www.dailyrecord.co.uk/news/politics/tory-msp-david-mundell-accuses-6771946#KFBBPYJ728oC4ias.97

[9] ibid

[10] http://www.dailyrecord.co.uk/news/politics/record-view-how-snp-use-5774496#FRZbkpMY2KsZC00v.97

[11] https://www.commonspace.scot/articles/998/alex-salmond-claims-smith-agreement-forbids-full-fiscal-autonomy-financial-black-hole

[12] http://www.bbc.co.uk/news/uk-scotland-31831857

[13] http://www.dailyrecord.co.uk/news/politics/john-swinney-not-just-want-7278956#CVVryg1tMAMUQFW6.97

[14] http://www.dailyrecord.co.uk/news/politics/new-powers-scottish-government-blocked-7274354#rlabs=42%20p$2#CimYYTsgtelGkw2u.97

[15] http://www.dailyrecord.co.uk/news/politics/record-view-its-time-cameron-7289761#y4hA166zPlHJUmXe.97

[16] ibid

[17] ibid

[18] ibid

[19] ibid

[20] http://www.britannica.com/topic/Whig-Party-England

[21] ibid

[22] http://www.infoplease.com/encyclopedia/history/conservative-party-british-political-party-the-rise-conservative-party.html

[23] http://www.liberalhistory.org.uk/history/liberal-unionists/

[24] https://en.wikipedia.org/wiki/Unionist_Party_(Scotland)#Merg

er_with_the_Conservative_Party
[25] http://www.bbc.co.uk/news/uk-politics-10518842
[26] http://www.scotsman.com/news/politics/kezia-dugdale-challenges-nicola-sturgeon-with-1p-income-tax-rise-plan-1-4018138
[27] https://www.eveningexpress.co.uk/pipe/news/scotland/evel-may-mean-end-of-barnett-formula/
[28] http://www.dailyrecord.co.uk/news/politics/record-view-tories-arent-shafting-7314774#rlabs=1%20rt$category%20p$4#DRHBBxl60iSeFGZv.97
[29] ibid
[30] Ibid
[31] http://www.dailyrecord.co.uk/news/politics/nicola-sturgeon-hails-historic-financial-7428736#ju7OfzRb6kVYUZCW.97
[32] http://news.stv.tv/politics/1343912-deal-reached-on-fiscal-framework-funding-arrangements/
[33] Ibid

Chapter 3

[1] http://www.telegraph.co.uk/news/politics/SNP/11514933/Nicola-Sturgeon-secretly-backs-David-Cameron.html
[2] http://www.dailyrecord.co.uk/news/politics/nicola-sturgeon-denies-explosive-claims-5455921#cKIpGOuXDTOI6bVD.97
[3] http://www.dailyrecord.co.uk/news/politics/meet-new-snp-candidate-ochil-5075268#rlabs=3%20rt$category%20p$2#Ij2mjHFhlSThGEtO.97
[4] ibid
[5] http://www.scotsman.com/news/tasmina-ahmed-sheikh-facing-questions-over-taxpayer-funded-charity-1-4000246
[6] http://www.dailyrecord.co.uk/news/politics/snp-mp-tasmina-ahmed-sheikh-7177441#Qur8X5IoBcifHPJq.97
[7] ibid
[8] I cannot give a link to a source since I am relating this from Tasmina Ahmed-Sheikh's tweet.
[9] Again, I can give no link for the reason outlined above.
[10] http://www.dailyrecord.co.uk/news/politics/how-can-michelle-thomson-sleep-6568971#d715Qmg6il1pREgt.97
[11] ibid
[12] ibid
[13] http://www.dailyrecord.co.uk/news/politics/snp-mp-michelle-thomson-perfectly-6541318#HHkrsmlLtYOgCvFd.97
[14] http://www.theguardian.com/technology/2015/aug/19/snp-mp-michelle-thomsons-data-hack-adultury-ashley-madison
[15] ibid
[16] http://order-order.com/2015/08/21/truth-about-mps-online-adultery-account/
[17] http://www.independent.co.uk/news/uk/politics/snp-politician-apologises-unreservedly-for-anti-semitic-tweet-a6732756.html
[18] http://www.bbc.co.uk/news/uk-scotland-scotland-politics-34807884
[19] http://www.independent.co.uk/news/uk/politics/snp-politician-apologises-unreservedly-for-anti-semitic-tweet-a6732756.html
[20] https://storify.com/InTheSoupAgain/a-bucket-of-charles-friths-s-racism
[21] change.org Petition for Sandra White MSP to resign
[22] http://yachad.org.uk/core-principles/
[23] http://www.dailyrecord.co.uk/news/politics/aide-snp-deputy-leader-stewart-7189092#KjrSo2JclirZguk1.97

[24] http://www.dailyrecord.co.uk/news/scottish-news/snp-councillor-accused-sending-racist-7203607#P53IY9RTQ3duhJU3.97

[25] http://www.dailyrecord.co.uk/news/scottish-news/snp-race-row-no2-holyrood-7222951#l3eGgV4wjczPXAPA.97

[26] ibid

[27] http://www.dailyrecord.co.uk/news/scottish-news/snp-holyrood-candidate-accused-racism-7296704#CJi05ysLOI6mCf2W.97

[28] http://www.thenational.scot/politics/turf-war-at-the-centre-of-racism-row-involving-snp-councillor-julie-mcanulty.13782?utm_medium=social&utm_source=Twitter&utm_campaign=Echobox&utm_term=Autofeed#link_time=1455606080

[29] http://www.eveningtimes.co.uk/news/13421750.Council_leader_reported_to_watchdog_over_contracts_row/

[30] http://www.dailyrecord.co.uk/news/scottish-news/snp-holyrood-candidate-accused-racism-7296704#CJi05ysLOI6mCf2W.97

[31] http://www.bbc.co.uk/news/uk-scotland-scotland-politics-35025601

[32] http://www.publications.parliament.uk/pa/cm/cmregmem/151130/boswell_philip.htm

[33] http://www.bbc.co.uk/news/uk-scotland-scotland-politics-35230380

[34] http://www.dailyrecord.co.uk/news/politics/snp-mp-centre-police-probe-6885561#pxGMHJUDwAV7eh64.97

[35] http://www.dailyrecord.co.uk/news/politics/natalie-mcgarry-handed-four-figure-6909180#dED4OmViCS7iKmv6.97

[36] http://aidankerr.com/2015/11/24/snp-ministers-office-manager-wfi-are-bullies-and-natalie-mcgarry-is-innocent/

[37] http://www.dailyrecord.co.uk/news/politics/natalie-mcgarry-handed-four-figure-6909180#RLY6CFTU3jM5BlLs.97

[38] http://www.dailyrecord.co.uk/news/politics/natalie-mcgarry-automatically-suspended-snp-6892903#eY5yqZldF5EMphq4.97

[39] http://www.dailyrecord.co.uk/news/politics/cash-probe-mp-natalie-mcgarry-6937901#pggRwA65ECSgOFd2.97

[40] http://wingsoverscotland.com/an-absence-of-clarity/

[41] http://www.dailyrecord.co.uk/news/politics/labour-find-half-missing-10k-6925066#VzdLcFzLfM2svMpG.97

[42] http://www.edinburghnews.scotsman.com/news/crime/half-of-missing-labour-cash-found-but-probe-goes-on-1-3962394
[43] http://www.dailymail.co.uk/news/article-3420296/Top-SNP-MP-MP-moonlights-500-day-NHS-surgeon-Party-s-health-spokesman-boosts-74-000-salary-working-cash-strapped-hospital.html
[44] ibid
[45] http://www.dailyrecord.co.uk/news/local-news/ayrshire-snp-health-guru-philippa-7262291#qsgmcGXORtLF3WMe.97
[46] http://www.dailyrecord.co.uk/news/local-news/nhs-ayrshire-arran-searches-abroad-7262618#7CB50C65cWXwX323.97
[47] http://www.dailyrecord.co.uk/news/politics/snp-party-members-among-14-7498347#Ks8G4RmHkUSmxgls.97
[48] ibid
[49] ibid
[50] http://www.dailyrecord.co.uk/news/scottish-news/cybernat-ran-online-campaign-accusing-6737578#MECFYl46Sz2dxz2W.97
[51] http://www.dailyrecord.co.uk/news/scottish-news/cybernat-troll-fined-1500-after-7305775#RiVBKi8yDspFdDZx.97

Chapter 4

[1] https://www.splcenter.org/fighting-hate/extremist-files/group/westboro-baptist-church

[2] http://www.huffingtonpost.co.uk/2016/01/16/westboro-baptist-church-david-bowie-dead-memorial-usa-cancer-child_n_8997566.html?utm_hp_ref=uk-entertainment&ir=UK+Entertainment&icid=mainggrid7%7Cuk%7Cdl2%7Csec3_lnk4%26pLid%3D420926

[3] ibid

[4] http://www.dailyrecord.co.uk/news/scottish-news/cybernat-trolls-take-twitter-abuse-7156522#pohrFYZex3EgSS2G.97

[5] ibid

[6] ibid

[7] http://www.theguardian.com/lifeandstyle/2010/sep/12/michelle-mone-lingerie-71-degrees-north

[8] ibid

[9] http://www.telegraph.co.uk/finance/markets/2820804/Michelle-Mone-the-Bra-Queen.html

[10] http://www.theguardian.com/lifeandstyle/2010/sep/12/michelle-mone-lingerie-71-degrees-north

[11] http://www.scotsman.com/news/world/underwear-tycoon-denies-sweat-shop-reports-1-523506

[12] http://www.scotsman.com/news/mone-hits-out-at-workers-rights-after-start-of-tribunal-1-719678

[13] http://www.bbc.co.uk/news/uk-scotland-scotland-politics-16779891

[14] http://www.dailyrecord.co.uk/news/politics/bra-tycoon-michelle-mone-takes-6639833#d7YOxWiQ5gXpjifu.97

[15] http://www.huffingtonpost.co.uk/2014/08/26/lingerie-tycoon-michelle-mone-cybernats_n_5714655.html

[16] http://www.itv.com/goodmorningbritain/news/internet-trolling-michelle-mone-will-francis

[17] http://www.theverge.com/2015/2/4/7982099/twitter-ceo-sent-memo-taking-personal-responsibility-for-the

[18] http://www.dailyrecord.co.uk/news/scottish-news/bra-tycoon-michelle-mone-quits-5740588#gJveMuRcAQ2krXcV.97

[19] http://www.dailyrecord.co.uk/entertainment/celebrity/bleating-bra-queen-michelle-mone-5795951#QqBDYuFer3AoppCE.97

[20] http://www.dailymail.co.uk/femail/article-3104020/Scotland-s-Bra-Queen-driven-home-vitriol-Sturgeon-s-CyberNats-real-

reason-millionaire-heading-south-words.html
[21] http://www.express.co.uk/news/uk/581228/Michelle-Mone-SNP-cybernats?_ga=1.171699552.1963804751.1433761254
[22] http://www.express.co.uk/celebrity-news/562824/Michelle-Mone-autobiography-My-Fight-To-The-Top-signing-Glasgow
[23] http://www.express.co.uk/news/uk/561309/michelle-mone-autobiography
[24] http://www.theguardian.com/business/2015/aug/16/michelle-mone-startup-tsar-ultimo-profile
[25] http://www.scotsman.com/news/euan-mccolm-scots-tory-cringe-over-michelle-mone-1-3859928
[26] http://www.dailyrecord.co.uk/news/scottish-news/michelle-mone-hits-back-twitter-6180264#MPTB1oyfdsxxjimw.97
[27] http://www.dailyrecord.co.uk/news/scottish-news/bra-tycoon-michelle-mone-quits-5740588#Pc1lsCRlg7oe1W0Y.97
[28] http://news.stv.tv/west-central/1330740-michelle-mone-takes-seat-house-of-lords-as-baroness-mone-of-mayfair/
[29] https://web.archive.org/web/20070527023912/http://www.cbc.ca:80/arts/story/2005/11/04/wyrdlawsuit_051104.html
http://www.canada.com/vancouversun/news/arts/story.html?id=ece18f65-1eb9-4829-9e2b-1d50a0dca298
[30] http://www.canada.com/vancouversun/news/arts/story.html?id=ece18f65-1eb9-4829-9e2b-1d50a0dca298
[31] http://www.scotsman.com/lifestyle/culture/books/the-jk-rowling-story-1-652114
[32] ibid
[33] http://www.telegraph.co.uk/culture/books/3666215/From-the-dole-to-Hollywood.html
http://www.scotsman.com/lifestyle/culture/books/the-jk-rowling-story-1-652114
[34] 'Harry Potter and the Philosopher's Stone' Chapter 3
[35] http://www.express.co.uk/news/uk/482638/Police-to-investigate-cybernat-abuse-aimed-at-JK-Rowling
[36] http://www.theguardian.com/commentisfree/2014/jun/12/cybernat-attack-jk-rowling-scottish-voters-online-abuse-scottish-independence
[37] http://www.dailyrecord.co.uk/news/politics/nicola-sturgeon-warns-cybernats-not-6659816#IYmH5FJ7o9cWR3qZ.97
[38] ibid
[39] ibid
[40] http://www.scotsman.com/news/politics/alex-salmond-gets-death-threats-online-1-3452908

[41] http://www.dailymail.co.uk/news/article-3346220/Tory-MP-voted-bomb-Syria-Facebook-death-threat-row-adding-unless-die-constituent-s-email.html
[42] http://blogs.spectator.co.uk/2015/08/frances-barber-blasts-cybernats-for-insulting-cilla-black/
[43] ibid
[44] ibid
[45] https://twitter.com/jem16_ed?lang=en-gb&lang=en-gb
[46] https://twitter.com/MrSuperAli?lang=en-gb
[47] http://www.dailymail.co.uk/news/article-3042846/JANET-STREET-PORTER-Death-threats-joke-ice-cream-exposed-sick-heart-SNP.html
[48] Ibid

Chapter 5

[1] http://www.dailyrecord.co.uk/news/scottish-news/bbc-refuse-send-staff-ibrox-6179565#XQHcS2MLXiTzIjlr.97

[2] http://vanguardbears.co.uk/article.php?i=91&a=rangers-withdraw-business-from-the-herald

[3] http://www.heraldscotland.com/sport/14231746.Apology__Spiers_on_Sport__December_30__2015/

[4] http://www.bbc.co.uk/news/uk-scotland-glasgow-west-35439391

[5] http://www.sportsjournalists.co.uk/journalism-news/regional-newspapers/two-columnists-leave-herald-over-rangers-apology/

[6] http://www.bbc.co.uk/news/uk-scotland-glasgow-west-35607032

[7] http://www.bbc.co.uk/news/uk-scotland-glasgow-west-35439391

[8] http://www.theguardian.com/books/2015/jul/23/jk-rowling-hedge-trimming-blamed-traffic-chaos-edinburgh-home

[9] http://www.telegraph.co.uk/culture/harry-potter/11757009/J-K-Rowling-hedge-trimming-causes-traffic-chaos-for-neighbours.html

[10] http://www.mirror.co.uk/3am/celebrity-news/jk-rowling-angers-neighbours-causing-6120695

[11] http://wingsoverscotland.com/jk-rowling-is-a-litigious-bully/

[12] http://www.theguardian.com/media/greenslade/2014/jan/31/jkrowling-dailymail

[13] http://www.dailyrecord.co.uk/news/local-news/trade-union-members-take-zero-7303383#0F3LjtJi6472vdfA.97

[14] http://www.dailyrecord.co.uk/news/uk-world-news/jk-rowling-destroys-snp-politician-7266360#boqDtbKxECyV1gbA.97

[15] ibid

[16] http://wingsoverscotland.com/the-tweets-you-wont-read/

[17] http://www.dailyrecord.co.uk/news/uk-world-news/jk-rowling-destroys-snp-politician-7266360#boqDtbKxECyV1gbA.97

[18] http://wingsoverscotland.com/the-tweets-you-wont-read/

[19] http://www.dailyrecord.co.uk/news/uk-world-news/jk-rowling-destroys-snp-politician-7266360#boqDtbKxECyV1gbA.97

[20] http://wingsoverscotland.com/jk-rowling-is-a-litigious-bully/

[21] http://www.dailyrecord.co.uk/news/uk-world-news/jk-

rowling-destroys-snp-politician-7266360#boqDtbKxECyV1gbA.97

[22] http://wingsoverscotland.com/the-tweets-you-wont-read/

[23] http://bellacaledonia.org.uk/2016/02/07/social-media-anti-social-misogyny/

[24] http://derekbateman.co.uk/2016/02/01/author-author/

[25] http://wingsoverscotland.com/jk-rowling-is-a-litigious-bully/

Chapter 6

[1] http://www.scotsman.com/news/politics/rise-scots-left-wing-electoral-alliance-launches-1-3872359
[2] ibid
[3] ibid
[4] http://www.dailyrecord.co.uk/news/politics/new-left-wing-coalition-rise-6349609#OJyGozi2ldREZIhC.97
[5] http://www.socialistworld.net/doc/7319
[6] http://www.rise.scot/rise-candidates-2016
[7] https://www.commonspace.scot/articles/3254/ross-ahlfeld-a-christian-socialist-reflection-on-rise-scotland
[8] http://www.dailyrecord.co.uk/news/scottish-news/new-left-wing-alliance-socialists-7217498#G2eRvsYZB8cTSrSB.97
[9] https://en.wikipedia.org/wiki/Cat_Boyd#Background
[10] http://alanbissett.com/about/
[11] https://en.wikipedia.org/wiki/Mike_Small_(author)
[12] http://wingsoverscotland.com/woman-buys-thing-with-own-money/
[13] http://leftproject.scot/2015/left-project-to-launch-rise/
[14] http://www.eveningtimes.co.uk/news/14226516.Tommy_Sheridan_will_quit_politics_if_he_loses_at_next_election/
[15] ibid
[16] http://www.socialistworld.net/doc/7319
[17] http://www.socialistparty.org.uk/articles/9019
[18] http://powerbase.info/index.php/Economic_League#Police_support
[19] ibid
[20] http://www.theguardian.com/commentisfree/2010/mar/18/undercover-police-infiltration-yre
[21] http://www.bbc.co.uk/news/uk-england-london-14439970
[22] http://aangirfan.blogspot.co.uk/2011/12/ira-run-by-spooks.html
[23] http://www.heraldscotland.com/opinion/14210075.Why_a_hectoring_online_fringe_is_putting_the_achievements_of_the_Yes_movement_at_risk/?ref=ar
[24] http://www.workersliberty.org/story/2010/09/06/jimmy-reid-%E2%80%93-people%E2%80%99s-stalinist
[25] http://www.wsws.org/en/articles/2010/08/reid-a25.html
[26] http://www.thecourier.co.uk/news/politics/twitter-row-erupts-between-msps-in-wake-of-organ-donation-vote-1.923673
[27] http://www.bbc.co.uk/news/live/uk-scotland-scotland-politics-

35521457
[28] http://www.thecourier.co.uk/news/politics/twitter-row-erupts-between-msps-in-wake-of-organ-donation-vote-1.923673
[29] ibid
[30] http://www.thecourier.co.uk/news/scotland/msps-vote-down-organ-donation-opt-out-system-1.923552
[31] http://www.dailyrecord.co.uk/news/politics/holyroods-organ-donation-vote-labelled-7355171#KluAodf2UZUvrHHq.97
[32] ibid
[33] http://www.theguardian.com/uk-news/2015/sep/18/scotland-rise-alliance-snp-holyrood
[34] http://www.scotsman.com/news/politics/rise-scots-left-wing-electoral-alliance-launches-1-3872359
[35] http://www.dailyrecord.co.uk/news/politics/gerry-hassan-snp-victory-assumed-7544748#cIE3rDOpMJWUy9Ed.97
[36] http://bellacaledonia.org.uk/tag/cat-boyd/
[37] http://www.heraldscotland.com/opinion/14210075.Why_a_hectoring_online_fringe_is_putting_the_achievements_of_the_Yes_movement_at_risk/?ref=ar

Chapter 7

[1] http://www.scotsman.com/news/homecoming-for-bruce-snp-brainwashing-1-774723

[2] http://www.theguardian.com/books/2012/oct/19/sansom-dominion-nightmare-nazi-britain

[3] http://www.antimoon.com/forum/t5221.htm

[4] http://www.itchy-coo.com/index.html

[5] http://www.amazon.co.uk/The-Sleekit-Tod-Fantastic-Scots/dp/1845021983/ref=pd_sim_14_2?ie=UTF8&dpID=518G65r0-eL&dpSrc=sims&preST=_AC_UL160_SR104%2C160_&refRID=1N9ETVMWP5X6A8WRHBVT

[6] ibid

[7] http://bellacaledonia.org.uk/2016/02/01/on-scots-language/

[8] ibid

[9] http://bellacaledonia.org.uk/2016/02/15/and-the-next-makar-is/

[10] ibid

[11] https://www.youtube.com/watch?v=HivJ4EosWS8

[12] http://myweb.tiscali.co.uk/epochmag/contents4/thistle1.html

[13] http://french.about.com/cs/francophonie/a/academie.htm

[14] http://bellacaledonia.org.uk/2016/02/01/on-scots-language/

[15] ibid

[16] http://www.dailyrecord.co.uk/news/scottish-news/gobbledygook-web-page-set-up-7497393#6M5Ei5IqFHkTkudW.97

[17] Ibid

Chapter 8

[1] http://www.dailyrecord.co.uk/news/scottish-news/homeless-man-who-suffers-depression-7289470#z6vyfcFo3JZDXbe5.97

[2] http://www.dailyrecord.co.uk/news/real-life/scots-mum-waiting-double-hand-7266279#Q3T2ucouGfgijWaQ.97

[3] http://www.scotsman.com/news/ministers-accused-of-cover-up-over-historic-sexual-abuse-1-3953482

[4] http://news.scotland.gov.uk/News/Inquiry-into-institutional-child-abuse-13b2.aspx

[5] http://www.eveningtimes.co.uk/news/14271284.Abuse_victims_to_keep_up_calls_for_inquiry_to_be_widened/

[6] http://www.scotsman.com/news/ministers-accused-of-cover-up-over-historic-sexual-abuse-1-3953482

[7] http://www.independent.co.uk/news/uk/this-britain/scottish-town-where-green-is-beyond-the-pale-981747.html

[8] http://archive.thetablet.co.uk/article/8th-july-1995/30/knights-go-to-war-the-knights-of-st-columba-in

[9] http://www.independent.co.uk/news/uk/labour-to-act-over-monklands-council-scandal-mp-to-heal-wounds-caused-by-allegations-against-local-1410968.html

[10] http://archive.thetablet.co.uk/article/19th-november-1994/28/abbey-passes-the-buck-buckfast-fortified-wine-has-

[11] http://www.heraldscotland.com/news/12071155.QC_rebuts__Monklandsgate_apos__claims_Report_finds_no_evidence_of_nepotism_or_religious_bias_over_district_council_apos_s_job_applicants/

[12] https://www.whatdotheyknow.com/request/cost_of_st_patricks_day_festivit#comment-29070

[13] http://www.independent.co.uk/news/uk/this-britain/scottish-town-where-green-is-beyond-the-pale-981747.html

[14] http://www.express.co.uk/news/uk/156765/Commission-out-to-target-Buckfast-ban

[15] http://www.dailyrecord.co.uk/news/local-news/irish-tricolour-fly-coatbridge-mark-7359007#WfkwAV747zSUiu95.97

[16] http://www.dailyrecord.co.uk/news/scottish-news/palestine-flag-flies-over-scots-3940647#twsQ9qlPUITXtf5H.97

[17] http://regimentalblues.com/articles/official-statement-14022016.html

[18] http://athousandflowers.net/2015/03/15/scotlands-shame-loyalist-bigots-hijack-st-patricks-day-in-glasgow/

[19] http://www.eveningtimes.co.uk/news/14278248.Irish_

Tricolour_plans_for_Scots_council_dead_in_the_water_as_Labour_announces_it_will_vote_against_1916_Rising_tribute/?ref=rss

[20] http://www.cumbernauld-news.co.uk/news/local-news/snp-councillors-behind-irish-flag-vote-1-4028944

[21] http://www.dailyrecord.co.uk/news/local-news/controversial-move-fly-irish-flag-7379225#74tgkQMiCwxjeqWw.97

[22] ibid

[23] http://www.northlanarkshire.gov.uk/index.aspx?articleid=9059

[24] http://www.dailyrecord.co.uk/news/scottish-news/revealed-scots-jail-drug-busts-7410363#rlabs=11%20rt$category%20p$6#adAKRCb0GDl3297d.97

[25] ibid

[26] ibid

[27] http://www.dailyrecord.co.uk/news/scottish-news/sauna-slave-hell-former-prostitute-7372268#LwwTCsyTCkKvEIxK.97

[28] ibid

[29] http://www.bbc.co.uk/news/uk-scotland-scotland-politics-18498858

[30] http://www.dailyrecord.co.uk/news/politics/msp-rhoda-grant-vows-to-continue-1129778#l3ClkJD7Jw20Aj6j.97

[31] http://www.dailyrecord.co.uk/news/politics/msp-urges-holyrood-change-law-7414888#5IkbUQpHBI4Ff0he.97

[32] http://www.scottish.parliament.uk/parliamentarybusiness/28877.aspx?SearchType=Simple&DateFrom=2/22/2016 12:00:00 AM&DateTo=2/22/2016 11:59:59 PM&SortBy=DateSubmitted&ResultsPerPage=10

[33] http://www.dailyrecord.co.uk/news/politics/msp-urges-holyrood-change-law-7414888#2KeXwImttR1HYhhH.97

Chapter 9

[1] http://www.dailymail.co.uk/news/article-3455752/It-s-George-Osborne-signals-start-referendum-campaign-David-Cameron-prepares-Saturday-Cabinet-Falklands.html

[2] http://www.express.co.uk/news/politics/646023/George-Galloway-Nigel-Farage-Grassroots-out-Eurosceptics-appearance-Kate-Hoey

[3] http://www.belfasttelegraph.co.uk/news/politics/nigel-farage-hits-back-over-flak-for-appearing-with-george-galloway-34471774.html

[4] ibid

[5] http://www.express.co.uk/news/politics/646023/George-Galloway-Nigel-Farage-Grassroots-out-Eurosceptics-appearance-Kate-Hoey

[6] https://www.youtube.com/watch?v=tCCjEs9zGoc

[7] http://grassrootsout.co.uk/articles/2016/2/2/liam-fox-calls-for-britain-to-leave-eu-and-become-an-independent-sovereign-nation-again

[8] ibid

[9] http://grassrootsout.co.uk/articles/2016/2/2/peter-bone-mp-perfectly-clear-that-the-pms-renegotiation-is-of-very-little-consequence

[10] http://www.bbc.co.uk/news/uk-politics-eu-referendum-35625694

[11] http://www.theguardian.com/politics/2016/feb/24/david-cameron-launches-tory-campaign-to-stay-in-the-eu

[12] http://www.independent.co.uk/news/business/news/eu-referendum-workers-employee-rights-maternity-sick-holiday-leave-pay-a6889226.html

[13] http://www.telegraph.co.uk/news/newstopics/eureferendum/10153786/EU-exit-could-cost-expats-their-pensions.html

[14] http://www.abc.net.au/news/2016-02-21/brexit-campaign-to-stay-in-european-union-gains-momentum/7187914

[15] http://www.independent.co.uk/news/uk/politics/britain-leaving-the-eu-could-lead-to-scottish-independence-william-hague-warns-a6784141.html

[16] http://www.shetnews.co.uk/features/scottish-independence-debate/9011-cameron-conspiracy-rumours-dispelled

[17] http://www.bbc.co.uk/news/uk-scotland-scotland-business-29739085

[18] http://www.bbc.co.uk/news/uk-scotland-north-east-orkney-

shetland-35568837
[19] ibid
[20] http://bellacaledonia.org.uk/2016/02/24/plan-b-for-europe/
[21] http://solidarity.scot/solidarity-position-on-europe/
[22] ibid
[23] http://solidarity.scot/feature/tommy-sheridan-launches-glasgow-campaign/
[24] http://files.heraldscotland.com/news/14226374.Tommy_Sheridan_will_quit_politics_if_he_loses_at_Holyrood_2016/?ref=rss
[25] http://www.1001portails.com/feeds_theguardian_com_theguardian_uk-news_rss-t-53760-36362357-referendum_tale_of_two_tories_leaves_me_cold_%7c_kevin_mckenna.html#.VtJfWbDctjp
[26] http://www.dailyrecord.co.uk/news/politics/snp-stalwart-jim-sillars-urges-7487129#uMcs2Chq5GMtxcyi.97
[27] http://www.express.co.uk/news/politics/648585/Nicola-Sturgeon-SNP-Scottish-EU-campaign-launch-London
[28] ibid
[29] ibid
[30] http://www.dailyrecord.co.uk/news/politics/snp-stalwart-jim-sillars-urges-7487129#uMcs2Chq5GMtxcyi.97
[31] http://www.bbc.co.uk/news/uk-politics-35616768
[32] http://www.telegraph.co.uk/news/newstopics/eureferendum/12167851/eu-referendum-david-cameron-faces-mps-after-boris-johnson-backs-brexit-live.html#update-20160222-1021
[33] http://www.dailymail.co.uk/news/article-3449390/Emma-Thompson-leads-luvvies-telling-Britain-stay-Europe-not-retreat-cake-filled-misery-laden-grey-old-island.html
[34] ibid
[35] http://www.express.co.uk/finance/city/616730/US-trade-rep-Michael-Froman-Brexit-trade-threats-used-to-work-for-European-Commission
[36] http://www.express.co.uk/news/politics/634716/EU-referendum-Tory-MP-Philip-Hollobone-Barack-Obama-Brexit
[37] http://www.express.co.uk/finance/city/615920/Peter-Hargreaves-why-he-backs-Brexit-why-Mark-Carney-should-keep-out?_ga=1.254862216.1409107088.1446405182
[38] http://cyprus-mail.com/2016/02/23/uk-expats-concerned-over-referendum-outcome/

[39] http://www.telegraph.co.uk/expat/money/eu-referendum-expats-step-up-in-campaign-amid-brexit-fears/
[40] http://www.thelocal.es/20150529/british-expat-fury-over-eu-referendum-snub
[41] http://www.theguardian.com/politics/2016/feb/12/barack-obama-plans-eu-referendum-intervention
[42] http://www.sovereignty.org.uk/features/articles/votes.html
[43] http://www.express.co.uk/news/uk/579698/EU-Britain-ban-migrants-referendum
[44] http://www.telegraph.co.uk/news/newstopics/eureferendum/11945477/Brexit-Block-non-UK-citizens-from-voting-in-EU-referendum-says-new-report.html
[45] http://www.dailyrecord.co.uk/news/politics/independence-referendum-figures-revealed-majority-5408163#rlabs=42%20p$6#lXQYCplcDtZgi2DU.97
[46] https://www.politicshome.com/party-politics/articles/story/labour-msps-be-given-free-vote-brexit
[47] http://www.ibtimes.co.uk/eu-referendum-brexit-group-claims-10-scottish-labour-msps-could-join-campaign-1535368

Chapter 10

[1] http://www.dailyrecord.co.uk/news/politics/record-view-john-swinney-chance-7437224#JsdSk10lMUEPF7Lo.97

[2] http://news.stv.tv/politics/1343912-deal-reached-on-fiscal-framework-funding-arrangements/

[3] http://www.dailyrecord.co.uk/news/politics/record-view-vow-gave-chance-7429193#aUsR4jXfW3yQ61hm.97

[4] http://www.bbc.co.uk/news/uk-scotland-scotland-politics-35479646

[5] http://metro.co.uk/2015/07/21/is-labour-ever-going-to-oppose-the-government-another-abstention-is-on-its-way-5306613/

[6] http://www.itv.com/news/granada/2015-07-21/labour-mp-why-i-voted-against-party-on-welfare-cuts/

[7] http://www.theguardian.com/politics/2015/jun/16/eu-referendum-campaign-labour-helps-cameron-dodge-eurosceptic-rebellion

[8] http://www.telegraph.co.uk/news/politics/labour/11860227/labour-leadership-election-results.html

[9] http://www.ibtimes.co.uk/labour-membership-hits-342000-jeremy-corbyn-attracts-left-wing-surge-support-1519841

[10] http://www.theguardian.com/politics/2015/aug/27/jeremy-corbyn-labour-membership-policy-leadership

[11] http://www.telegraph.co.uk/news/politics/labour/11799596/Labour-faces-annihilation-under-Jeremy-Corbyn-Tony-Blair-warns-in-dramatic-late-intervention.html

[12] http://www.bbc.co.uk/news/uk-politics-34967024

[13] http://www.huffingtonpost.co.uk/2016/01/13/trident-jeremy-corbyn-free-vote-jonathan-ashworth_n_8972742.html

[14] http://www.bbc.co.uk/news/uk-scotland-scotland-politics-29996711

[15] http://www.monbiot.com/2010/11/22/the-uks-odious-debts/

[16] http://www.gov.scot/Topics/Government/local-government/17999/counciltax

[17] http://www.eveningtimes.co.uk/news/14317708.Council_tax_changes_Impact_on_Glasgow/

[18] http://www.dab-vjb.gov.uk/council-tax/bands-by-council-and-ward/east-dunbartonshire-bandings-per-ward/

[19] ibid

[20] https://en.wikipedia.org/wiki/East_Dunbartonshire#Demographics

[21] http://www.dab-vjb.gov.uk/council-tax/bands-by-council-and-

ward/east-dunbartonshire-bandings-per-ward/
[22] http://www.eastdunbarton.gov.uk/residents/council-tax/council-tax-bands-charges-appeals
[23] https://www.glasgow.gov.uk/index.aspx?articleid=17021
[24] http://www.dailyrecord.co.uk/news/politics/council-tax-freeze-ends-sturgeon-7477879#4KTyEdBiF7WkZEhd.97
[25] ibid
[26] http://www.expressandstar.com/business/uk-money/2016/03/02/sturgeon-announces-end-of-council-tax-freeze-and-higher-bills-for-bands-e-to-h/
[27] http://www.dailyrecord.co.uk/news/politics/council-tax-freeze-ends-sturgeon-7477879#LJYxAcJHubKyib4o.97
[28] http://news.stv.tv/politics/1344918-top-council-tax-bands-set-to-increase-says-nicola-sturgeon/

Chapter 11

[1] http://www.dailyrecord.co.uk/news/scottish-news/deputy-first-minister-john-swinney-7467887#2KYZSLECkXqqpROx.97

[2] http://news.sky.com/story/1330438/scotland-vote-will-impact-northern-ireland

[3] http://grassrootsout.co.uk/articles/2016/2/2/liam-fox-calls-for-britain-to-leave-eu-and-become-an-independent-sovereign-nation-again

[4] http://whitegenocideproject.com/whites-should-leave-zimbabwe-says-president-mugabe/

[5] http://www.independent.co.uk/news/uk/home-news/white-britons-could-be-minority-by-2066-2137329.html

[6] http://www.theguardian.com/commentisfree/2007/mar/16/watchingdavidcoleman1

[7] http://www.educationscotland.gov.uk/higherscottishhistory/migrationandempire/experienceofimmigrants/irish.asp

[8] http://www.dailyrecord.co.uk/sport/football/isnt-there-enough-to-worry-about-without-beating-991268#kYp2PuhLJLqxVv6t.97

[9] http://www.bbc.co.uk/news/magazine-21791038

[10] http://www.prisonreformtrust.org.uk/ProjectsResearch/Race

[11] http://scottishlaw.blogspot.co.uk/2011/10/sectarian-scotland-reports-on-prison.html

[12] http://www.brin.ac.uk/2011/catholics-in-scottish-prisons/

[13] http://www.heraldscotland.com/news/13107523.Scotland__hostile_to_Catholics____genuine_response_to_prejudice_or_lingering_sense_of_victimhood_/

[14] https://www.commonspace.scot/articles/3444/12-things-you-didn-t-know-about-cat-boyd-kittycatboyd

[15] http://www.gov.scot/About/reviewofteacheremployment/reviewteam/isabelleboyd

[16] http://www.localnewsglasgow.co.uk/tag/cat-boyd/

[17] http://thirdforcenews.org.uk/blogs/im-no-citizen-smith-cat-boyd-on-why-she-campaigns

[18] https://en.wikipedia.org/wiki/Cat_Boyd

[19] http://www.thenational.scot/comment/cat-boyd-im-proud-of-my-irish-background-why-cant-glasgow-celebrate-st-patricks-day-like-everyone-else.14404

[20] ibid

[21] ibid

[22] http://www.dailyrecord.co.uk/news/politics/independence-

referendum-figures-revealed-majority-5408163#rlabs=42%20p$6#soBKlrpaUiR97d3E.97

[23] http://www.thenational.scot/comment/cat-boyd-im-proud-of-my-irish-background-why-cant-glasgow-celebrate-st-patricks-day-like-everyone-else.14404

[24] http://www.gov.scot/Topics/archive/law-order/sectarianism-action-1/football-violence/bill

[25] http://news.stv.tv/west-central/1344818-celtic-call-for-offensive-behaviour-act-to-be-repealed/

[26] http://www.telegraph.co.uk/news/uknews/scotland/ 9991384/Sheriff-makes-mincemeat-of-ill-considered-law-making.html

[27] http://www.heraldscotland.com/sport/14218393.SPFL_to_investigate_unacceptable_conduct_following_Ibrox_and_Tynecastle_matches/

[28] http://www.dailyrecord.co.uk/opinion/sport/rangers-record-fc-billy-boys-7093686#2jwDjU1e8QUIgbVb.97

Chapter 12

[1] http://www.dailyrecord.co.uk/news/politics/independence-referendum-legendary-political-commentator-3802346#7bxr84qyERpLAjm2.97

[2] http://www.dailyrecord.co.uk/authors/torcuil-crichton/#eFAAlw2jpw35jXCq.97

[3] https://www.facebook.com/torcuil

[4] https://www.linkedin.com/in/torcuil-crichton-1944aba

[5] http://www.gaelic-arts.com/gd/about-us/what-we-do/our-work/people/board-of-directors/

[6] http://www.gaelic-arts.com/gd/about-us/what-we-do/our-work/

[7] http://www.dailyrecord.co.uk/news/politics/shock-report-says-holyrood-find-7513391#pomCUT3ZKWoMmqBR.97

[8] http://www.dailyrecord.co.uk/news/politics/torcuil-crichton-its-no-surprise-7355295#3rkuK2emYfeC97bC.97

[9] http://www.independent.co.uk/news/uk/politics/generalelection/general-election-2015-scottish-tory-candidate-alexander-stewart-on-tactical-voting-as-snp-surges-10220882.html

[10] http://www.telegraph.co.uk/news/uknews/scotland/12186798/Natalie-McGarry-MP-facing-legal-action-over-holocaust-tweet.html

[11] http://www.scotlandinunion.co.uk/

[12] https://www.youtube.com/watch?v=XLk5C-zq8Do

[13] http://www.scotlandinunion.co.uk/whoweare

[14] http://www.scotlandinunion.co.uk/tactical_voting_an_introduction

[15] http://www.scotlandinunion.co.uk/a_charter_for_holyrood

[16] http://researchbriefings.parliament.uk/ResearchBriefing/Summary/SN05262

[17] http://www.scotlandinunion.co.uk/glasgow_supporters_event_alastair_cameron_s_speech

[18] ibid

[19] ibid

[20] https://en.wikipedia.org/wiki/Mike_Small_(author)

[21] http://bellacaledonia.org.uk/2014/04/01/where-is-alexander-linklater/

[22] https://bampotsutd.wordpress.com/2016/03/08/lemon-water/

[23] https://bampotsutd.wordpress.com/2015/03/23/mike-bella-a-media-parasite-in-nationalist-clothing/

[24] http://www.express.co.uk/news/uk/267729/Jackie-Baillie-too-

posh-to-be-Labour-leader
[25] ibid
[26] http://www.scottish.parliament.uk/parliamentarybusiness/15519.aspx
[27] http://www.ibtimes.co.uk/holyrood-rejects-trident-renewal-full-list-msps-who-voted-against-scrapping-nuclear-deterrent-1527048
[28] http://www.dailyrecord.co.uk/news/scottish-news/neil-findlay-msp-dont-sell-6601467#zYohvDgJourfEmY7.97
[29] http://www.scotsman.com/news/jackie-baillie-weed-out-parties-financial-fantasy-1-3664722
[30] Ibid

Chapter 13

[1] https://twitter.com/RuthDavidsonMSP/status/707519737127895040?lang=en-gb

[2] http://www.gov.scot/Topics/Statistics/Browse/Economy/GERS

[3] http://www.dailyrecord.co.uk/news/politics/great-eckscape-independent-scotland-would-7528322#uqrr5rKMl8lYUWFu.97

[4] http://www.bbc.co.uk/news/uk-scotland-scotland-politics-35757787

[5] http://www.dailyrecord.co.uk/news/politics/great-eckscape-independent-scotland-would-7528322#lI4L4vVM8mLt9iY4.97

[6] http://www.bbc.co.uk/news/uk-scotland-scotland-business-29946267

[7] http://www.businessforscotland.co.uk/new-figures-confirm-that-scotland-would-have-been-8-3-billion-better-off-an-independent-country/

[8] ibid (comments section)

[9] http://www.bbc.co.uk/news/uk-scotland-scotland-politics-35757787

[10] ibid

[11] http://linkis.com/www.theguardian.com/MGoc2

[12] http://blogs.spectator.co.uk/2016/03/the-scottish-governments-own-figures-demolish-the-economic-case-for-independence/

[13] http://www.gov.scot/Publications/2016/03/3692/downloads

[14] http://www.insidehousing.co.uk/tenancies/majority-of-new-housing-benefit-claimants-in-work/6521183.article

[15] http://www.theguardian.com/news/datablog/2013/jan/08/uk-benefit-welfare-spending

[16] https://www.gov.uk/government/collections/dwp-statistical-summaries

[17] http://www.gov.scot/Topics/Health/Services/Mental-Health

[18] http://www.youngminds.org.uk/training_services/policy/policy_in_the_uk/camhs_policy_in_scotland

[19] http://www.wellscotland.info/priorities/addressing-common-mental-health-problems/depression

[20] http://www.scotpho.org.uk/health-wellbeing-and-disease/mental-health/data/deprivation

[21] http://www.dailyrecord.co.uk/news/politics/kezia-dugdale-tories-gonna-tory-7551377#embIJ1sZkoVG86ig.97

[22] http://blogs.spectator.co.uk/2016/03/the-scottish-governments-own-figures-demolish-the-economic-case-for-independence/

[23] http://www.express.co.uk/news/politics/651510/Let-them-leave-Annoyed-French-politicians-Brexit-EU-referendum
[24] ibid
[25] https://www.eveningexpress.co.uk/pipe/news/scotland/nicola-sturgeon-concerned-by-eu-referendum-narrow-focus/
[26] http://www.telegraph.co.uk/news/uknews/scottish-independence/11862457/Nicola-Sturgeon-SNP-to-name-conditions-for-second-independence-referendum-in-2016-manifesto.html
[27] http://www.scotsman.com/news/politics/thousands-sign-petition-opposing-a-second-indyref-1-4067912

Chapter 14

[1] http://www.huffingtonpost.co.uk/entry/bbc-question-time-dundee-episode-producers-defend-audience-over-tory-andbrexit-bias-claims_uk_56e2f9cbe4b03fb88eddb872?utm_hp_ref=uk-news&icid=maing-grid7%7Cuk%7Cdl2%7Csec1_lnk2%26pLid%3D438938

[2] ibid

[3] ibid (comments section)

[4] http://wingsoverscotland.com/what-are-the-odds/

[5] http://wingsoverscotland.com/the-cream-of-the-crop/

[6] http://www.phoenix45.org/?p=263

[7] http://ekla.in/trends/kathy-wiles.html

[8] http://www.kirriemuirherald.co.uk/news/local-headlines/labour-announce-kathy-wiles-as-angus-candidate-1-3451999

[9] http://www.scotsman.com/news/politics/labour-candidate-resigns-over-hitler-youth-tweet-1-3462378

[10] http://www.bbc.co.uk/news/uk-scotland-scotland-politics-28106688

[11] http://www.kirriemuirherald.co.uk/news/local-headlines/labour-announce-kathy-wiles-as-angus-candidate-1-3451999

[12] http://wingsoverscotland.com/the-new-socialist/

[13] ibid

[14] http://www.thecourier.co.uk/news/local/dundee/bbc-question-time-comes-from-dundee-tonight-1.928233

[15] http://www.thecourier.co.uk/news/local/dundee/question-time-accent-row-does-dundee-no-favours-claims-resident-1.928831

[16] Ibid

Chapter 15

[1] http://www.upi.com/Business_News/Energy-Industry/2016/03/08/Oil-rallies-beyond-the-40-per-barrel-mark/6801457445558/

[2] http://www.dailyrecord.co.uk/news/scottish-news/revealed-msps-kept-silent-human-7548439#O8xQ7tikgiRkg38f.97

[3] Ibid

[4] http://www.dailyrecord.co.uk/news/politics/education-secretary-angela-constance-under-7605208#ch5qgBAETkHEKBCt.97

[5] ibid

Printed in Great Britain
by Amazon